OUNCES
OF
WISDOM

KENNETH W. OOSTING

GOD'S PLAN FOR SERVICE

Dr. Richard K. Smith, Editor

BALBOA.PRESS

A DIVISION OF HAY HOUSE

Balboa Press books may be ordered through booksellers or by contacting:

Balboa Press
A Division of Hay House
1663 Liberty Drive
Bloomington, IN 47403
www.balboapress.com
1 (877) 407-4847

Because of the dynamic nature of the Internet, any web addresses or links contained in this book may have changed since publication and may no longer be valid. The views expressed in this work are solely those of the author and do not necessarily reflect the views of the publisher, and the publisher hereby disclaims any responsibility for them.

The author of this book does not dispense medical advice or prescribe the use of any technique as a form of treatment for physical, emotional, or medical problems without the advice of a physician, either directly or indirectly. The intent of the author is only to offer information of a general nature to help you in your quest for emotional and spiritual well-being. In the event you use any of the information in this book for yourself, which is your constitutional right, the author and the publisher assume no responsibility for your actions.

Any people depicted in stock imagery provided by Getty Images are models, and such images are being used for illustrative purposes only.
Certain stock imagery © Getty Images.

Scripture taken from the King James Version of the Bible.

Scripture taken from the New King James Version®. Copyright © 1982 by Thomas Nelson. Used by permission. All rights reserved.

Scripture quotations taken from The Holy Bible, New International Version® NIV® Copyright © 1973 1978 1984 2011 by Biblica, Inc. TM. Used by permission. All rights reserved worldwide.

Printed in the United States of America.

ISBN: 978-1-9822-3937-4 (sc)
ISBN: 978-1-9822-3939-8 (hc)
ISBN: 978-1-9822-3938-1 (e)

Library of Congress Control Number: 2019919623

Balboa Press rev. date: 12/17/2019

Are you a person who is a thinker? Are you a person who wants to relate well with other people? Are you a person who wants to advance in your career? Are you a person who wants to live out Biblical values in your life and family? If you are answering these questions with a "yes", you must read AND digest the contents of this book. This is a book you must read when you are wide awake. There are no wasted words. Every word and every concept counts.

The author, Dr. Kenneth W. Oosting, brings an illustrative career and life to this volume. He has a PhD. and has been working many years in academia as a faculty member and administrator. As his final accomplishment, Dr. Oosting, along with his wife, owned an academic consulting firm, Oosting and Associates, where he served as president. I worked for Dr. Oosting for a period of ten years. The primary expertise of the consulting firm was to assist colleges and universities across North America to set up and manage adult degree completion programs. This type of academic program enabled working adults to come back to a program specifically designed to help them complete their undergraduate degree. Dr. Oosting was no doubt the lead authority on this kind of academic endeavor.

As part of his consulting work, Dr. Oosting wrote and edited curriculum for the adult programs. In working with him in this writing and editing, I learned how precise and concise Dr. Oosting was in his writing. This book is an example of Dr. Oosting's skill in examining a significant number of topics in a very detailed yet concise manner. He asks significant questions to assist the reader in thinking through the concepts presented. And then Dr. Oosting will bring to bear what Biblical truths apply to the issues he examines.

Dr. Oosting is a committed Christian and always seeks to use pertinent Scripture to relate to the subject areas he is discussing. It is refreshing that Dr. Oosting, who is not a minister nor is seminary trained, can bring Biblical truth to bear upon the matters he presents. This volume will make you think. This volume will help you to better relate to people at every level of your life. This volume will help you to be better equipped to deal with challenges of the working world. Most importantly, this volume will help you to apply Biblical guidelines to your life as you seek to grow as a person, be a leader in your family, and deal appropriately with the general public.

Warning, you may think about things you have not thought through before. Fear not, thou shalt be challenged and changed!!

Richard K. Smith, D.Miss.
Pataskala, Ohio

GOD'S PLAN FOR SERVICE

Established in 2008, the weekly programs are broadcast on radio, sent by email to a mailing list and appear monthly in the Nashville Christian Family magazine. The organization is 501c3 with the IRS and is a nonprofit Tennessee corporation guided by a four member Board of Directors. You may add your name to the email list at no cost by sending your name and email address to kwo@oosting.com or contacting any Board member. The mission of GPS is to encourage people to think about ways in which their life might be both more personally rewarding and pleasing to God. The members of the Board of Directors at the time of publication are:

Tom Andrews, Franklin, Tennessee
Dan Pearson, Byron Center, Michigan
Richard K. Smith, Pataskala, Ohio
Kenneth W. Oosting, Brentwood, Tennessee

God's Plan for Service began in 2008 with weekly radio broadcasts two minutes in length and designed to encourage people to think about the Christian faith as it applies to our daily lives. Thus admonitions from the Bible along with motivation and inspiration to live the life God would have us carry out on a daily basis became the theme. In time, sending the program by email to interested persons was started and this now goes out at no cost to the subscribers every Monday. You can add your name to this list by sending us your name and email address. There is no cost.

God's Plan for Service is a nonprofit organization guided by a four member Board of Directors. It is financially supported through donations that are tax deductible in the USA. The organization has no paid staff with its primary expense being radio time. Contributions may be sent to the address below to support this ministry. GPS is based in Brentwood (Williamson County), Tennessee next to Nashville, Tennessee. When the organization started I was President of Williamson Christian College. When I retired from that role in 2009, GPS continued and now reaches a larger audience through radio, emails each week and monthly in the Nashville Christian Family magazine.

The contents of this book were selected from the weekly programs over eleven years. Some 131 of these programs were selected to be a part of this book. The selection was based in part on how well a particular topic contributed to the title of the book, *Ounces of Wisdom*. New programs continue to be written and recorded at WAKM in Franklin, TN where the time and support of Tom Lawrence has been instrumental in the program's success.

There are themes in the teachings of Jesus that are emphasized in this book. The ideas for the programs come from many sources ranging from the Bible to secular sources, both historical and contemporary. The key has been whether the source has something to say that the reader or listener could use to make life more bountiful personally as well as pleasing to God.

You are encouraged to think more deeply about what God has in store for you and where you need to step up to fulfill the gifts and opportunities God has provided. Each of us has an impact on others which should be considered each day. This impact allows each of us to multiply our positive and faithful efforts to make the world around us a better one. We should seek to utilize our gifts in an effort to reach our potential while at the same time being a role model to help others reach their potential (their excellence). The more we live our lives pleasing to God, the closer we are to Him and the more we are prepared for life eternal with Him.

The work of the Board of God's Plan for Service which commissioned this book has been appreciated. A special appreciation is to Dr. Richard K. Smith for serving as Editor. His richness of thoughts and providing many of the Bible references has tied the essays more closely to the Bible.

Comments or questions may be sent to me at the address below. May the love of God permeate every thought and deed in your life.

Kenneth W. Oosting, Ph.D.
Brentwood, TN 37027
kwo@oosting.com

God's Plan for Service
1226 Knox Valley Drive
Brentwood, TN 37027

WISDOM

What is wisdom? Later programs will address wisdom and courage as well as wisdom and confidence. Wisdom is the combining of information, perspective, insight, values, emotion, interest in sharing as well as being sufficiently articulate in expressing a thought that others can hear or read the thought and realize that they now see the issue(s) much more clearly. Wisdom means seeing the deeper meaning as well as its implications. Wisdom is not the same as intelligence as seen in some very bright people who seldom discover wisdom and some simple people who might share precious nuggets of wisdom.

Let's look at each of those characteristics and then how they combine to create wisdom. First, information. There is nothing on which to express wisdom unless there is a subject matter and some information about that subject matter, however small or large. Wisdom involves reflecting on that information or data.

Second, perspective means a way of looking at something. A wise person has a perspective that might not even occur to most of us and helps to create an insight others do not have. An example would be the way Benjamin Franklin looked at lightning. He saw something there that others did not see (no pun intended).

Values are the third aspect of wisdom. Values tell us what is important in the world and explains our belief, our faith system. While not everyone believes in God, everyone believes in something, even if it is just the principle of gravity. This value system affects our perspective as well as our interests and our motivation. Without it there would be no desire to express wisdom and probably not a desire to discover it.

Fourth on this list is emotion. By emotion we mean an interest in life and what it offers. It is what stirs us. All people have emotion and most of us keep it under control. Under control, it moves us beyond knowledge to insight.

Fifth is the interest in sharing wisdom with others. This interest must be based on wanting others to benefit from our thinking, our conclusions. Maybe we will benefit as well as Franklin did with electricity.

Sixth is the factor that could cause all of the other efforts to come to naught. We have to be able to express wisdom in a fashion that can be understood by a multitude of others. Jesus was able to do this. Albert Einstein explained the Theory of Relativity in a manner that others could say, "How come I didn't see that?" Wisdom involves taking the most complex aspects of life and reducing them to simple terms. Theology, the study of the relationship between man and God, is very complex. However, John 3:16 reduces it to very simple terms as does the second Chapter of Acts.

What should you do about wisdom when you discover it? Opinions are everywhere; wisdom is seldom heard. Wisdom is not inherently good. You still must apply your value system to it to determine whether it is a flag to follow. In 1 Kings 3:12 Solomon is given a "wise and discerning heart." Each of us should seek no less.

STUDY QUESTIONS

1. Define what you think wisdom is.
2. Identify a person who you think has wisdom and shares it with others. What are the characteristics of this person? What experiences has he or she had? What is the nature of the wisdom they share?
3. What is the difference between wisdom and personal opinion?

28A

"Wise men profit more from fools than fools from wise men; for the wise men shun the mistakes of fools, but fools do not imitate the successes of the wise." Cato the Elder (234-149 B C)

"Wisdom comes from two sources. The first is careful study of God's word, pursuing the twins of doctrine and law. The second is knowledge gained from the experience of putting God's ways into practice." Dr. R. C. Sproul

For the Lord gives wisdom; from his mouth come knowledge and understanding. He holds success in store for the upright, he is a shield to those whose walk is blameless, for he guards the course of the just and protects the way of his faithful ones. Proverbs 2:6-8

"Be kind to one another, forgiving each other, just as Christ God forgave you" Ephesians 4:32

"In politics, if you want something said, ask a man. If you want anything done, ask a woman." Prime Minister Margaret Thatcher

"The most important decision you will ever make is about eternity." Rev. Billy Graham

"Always vote for a principle, though you vote alone, and you may cherish the sweet reflection that your is never lost." President John Quincy Adams

"Let us not seek the Republican answer or the Democratic answer, but the right answer. Let us not seek to fix the blame for the past. Let us accept our own responsibility for the future." President John F. Kennedy

"Talking about someone who makes you happy actually makes you happy." Elizabeth Scott

CONTENTS

CHAPTER ONE

WISDOM AND PERSONAL CHARACTER

Love, Character, Discernment, Seeking Wisdom, Compassion, Courage, Humility, Discipline, Conviction, Pride, Integrity, Clean Hearts, Being Articulate, Virtue, Perseverance, Knowing Right From Wrong, Convenience, Honesty

CHARACTER

Let's talk about building and having character. Romans 5:3-5 tells us:

> Not only so, but we also rejoice in our sufferings, because we know that suffering produces perseverance; perseverance, character; and character hope. And hope does not disappoint us, because God has poured out his love into our hearts by the Holy Spirit, whom he has given us.

Paul is talking about perseverance in the pursuit of those behaviors that would be within God's will. These are positive acts, grounded in love, and focused on praising God and serving others. If we persevere in the pursuit of these lofty behaviors, we will build character. We tend to use the term character meaning good character. A definition of character (vocabulary. com) is "the inherent complex of attributes that determines a person's moral and ethical actions and reactions." So good character means a person of high moral standards.

When we have character, what is it that we as Christians have? The love of God and his son Jesus Christ are paramount. Then there must be love of others and even of self. There must be a desire to live a life as close to the life of Jesus

Christ as possible while being obedient to the commands we find in the Bible. Character means following the moral standards mentioned in the Bible. When we sin, we must ask God for forgiveness. We must read and know our Bible and enter into daily prayer. We must have a passion for living out our faith through all that we say, think and do in our relationships with others and the rest of God's creation. It must be evident to others that we are Christians.

The last part of Paul's statement is that character will lead to hope. Hope is what sets aside the Christian from the non-believer. We have the hope of eternal life in Heaven instead of Hell. But to have that hope we must first persevere in living the Christian life and demonstrate Christian character. Non-believers have no hope for a positive eternal life because they hold to the assumption that there is no life after death or that everyone actually gets into Heaven.

Character is associated with integrity. A person with integrity is one who is what that person purports (claims) to be. There is no hidden agenda, no false pretense of being a person of different values. A person of high integrity and high moral character will stand firm in their values. The closer one is to God, the more likely that the person will have high integrity and good character. High integrity and good character are essentials for Christians. Paul said that perseverance is needed to provide good character. Do you have that perseverance?

STUDY QUESTIONS

1. What do you persevere in doing or saying? Is it in keeping with the Bible?
2. Following the message above, the essentials of character are given. If you are lacking in one or more of the qualities mentioned by Paul, what are those qualities and what are you doing about it?
3. What can you do to help build character and integrity in other people?

211A

INTEGRITY

Stephen W. Vannoy is quoted as saying:

> Integrity is how you act when no one is watching, when no one knows what you are doing. It is always telling the truth, clearing up misconceptions or partial truths. It's never knowingly hurting anybody or anything. Integrity is keeping our commitments.

When there is no difference between the person we claim to be and the person we really are, we are said to have integrity. Integrity means being transparent, not having ulterior motives, being of high standards and virtue. When we claim to be a person of high morals, interested in other people, dependable, relying on the truth as we understand it, we are looked up to in society. Others feel they can depend on us. If we fail even once, our integrity is likely to be forever questioned. As a result, to be known as a person of integrity is a high honor and most people want to be seen as such a person.

However, it is tempting to cut corners, not to tell the whole truth, or to embellish or diminish the truth in order to have a short-term gain. For example, if we are selling a used car to another person, how honestly would we describe the car we are selling? If we are applying for a position, we want to appear to be just the person for the job. Would we alter the facts just a little in order to get the job? Employers can hire a person lacking skills and then provide skill training but a person without integrity is never a good job candidate.

Being careless can cause a person of integrity to be questioned. To protect our integrity, we must be careful in everything we do or communicate to ensure that it accurately reflects the person we are. A person of integrity is always seeking the truth as the basis for action. When you act, be sure you are on solid ground. If the basis on which you act crumbles, your integrity will be questioned.

The benefits of being a person of integrity means we are able to be at peace with ourselves. We are not troubled with something we said or did that was not completely honest. We accomplish more because we are trusted by others. But to be a person of integrity we must in fact <u>be</u> the person we claim to be 100% of the time.

God knows everything about us. He knows if we are a person of integrity and <u>we</u> know it as well. Remember Proverbs 11:3: "The integrity of the upright guides them, but the unfaithful are destroyed by their duplicity." Cutting corners is never worth any possible short-term gain. Do people see <u>you</u> as a person of integrity?

STUDY QUESTIONS

1. How would you define integrity?
2. In what situations is your integrity most likely to be tested?
3. Has the lack of integrity in another person affected you? 46A

Wanting to be liked can get in the way
of the truth." Delia Ephron

"Blessed are the pure in heart: for they
shall see God." Matthew 5:8

"Set an example of good works yourself with integrity
and dignity in your teaching." Titus 2:7

ABSOLUTE HONESTY

Most of us are comfortable with the concept of honesty. We want our children, our co-workers, our boss, people at church and others to be honest with us. That means we want them to tell us the truth, the facts as they are known to them. At the same time, we recognize the need for us to be honest with others.

This is different from an error in which we communicate something not true but that which we thought was true but in fact was not. Unless we know the facts for sure, we need to avoid passing off what we think to be true as fact without a doubt. We do this by saying something like "To the best of my knowledge" or "I think" to qualify our words when we are not sure the information we have is currently accurate.

Honesty is something we expect and want from others. It is tempting, however, to think that <u>we</u> can shade the truth as we communicate with others even though we would be upset if someone else did that to us. We might use rationalization to justify our telling a "white lie" or communicating something that is only 95% true. Why would we do this? It might be to protect us from having to accept responsibility for what has happened, it might be an ego move to make us look better or it might be for personal gain (financial or otherwise).

Absolute honesty, on the other hand, means just that. Absolute means with no exceptions and all of the time. It might require us to be silent at times because we don't know all of the facts. You might argue that there are some things best left unsaid. That's true. We don't need to continually point out the mistakes of others. There is value in the adage, "If you can't say something good, keep your silence." Absolute honesty requires that when we <u>do</u> speak or write, we know what we are communicating is true, without exceptions.

Are you willing to communicate only with absolute honesty? Remember the Word of God to us in Proverbs 12:22: "The Lord detests lying lips, but he delights in people who are trustworthy."

STUDY QUESTIONS

1. Which is likely to have absolute honesty: a comment by a friend or the national news?
2. Our personal temptation is to say something that we think is true but we cannot support it with facts although we don't qualify the statement leading others to think it is done in absolute honesty. Have you ever done this?
3. When we pray, are we absolutely honest with God or do we rationalize and find excuses?

49

"If your conscience is bothering you, fix it by doing the right thing." Anonymous

"Whoever is careless with the truth in small matters cannot be trusted with important matters." Albert Einstein

"In essence, if we want to control our lives we must take control of our consistent actions. It's not what we do once in a while that shapes our lives, but what we do consistently." Tony Robbins

"Do not be anxious about anything, but in every situation, by prayer and petition, with thanksgiving, present your requests to God." Philippians 4:6

"The tongue of the wise adorns knowledge, but the mouth of the fool gushes folly." Proverbs 15:2

PRINCIPLES AND PREFERENCES

We make decisions every waking hour based on our values. Our values change slightly as we go through life (for example, riding a bicycle was important at age 10 but not at age 20 for most of us). Our values are made up of principles and preferences. It is essential that we understand the difference between them.

Principles tend to become more firm as we mature and age due to the number of decisions we must make. Principles are not subject to compromise or negotiation. An example of a principle would be "I believe in God." Another example might be "I will always be honest." Whenever we make a decision, we consider whether a principle is involved. If a principle is involved, our decision is based on that principle (or possibly several principles). In Philippians 4:8 we are told our principles should be based on "whatever is true, whatever is noble, whatever is right, whatever is pure, whatever is lovely, whatever is admirable – if anything is excellent or praiseworthy . . ."

If no principle is involved (e.g. the decision of whether to have oatmeal or Cheerios for breakfast), then our decision is based on our preferences. Preferences are open to negotiation and compromise. If someone else wants the last of the Cheerios, we can have something else for breakfast based on a lesser preference.

The importance of this is that we should never compromise a principle but that we should be ready to compromise our preferences in order to get along better with others. Do you know the difference between your principles and your preferences?

STUDY QUESTIONS

1. List at least five of your principles.
2. List at least five of your preferences.
3. To what extent do you live according to your principles?

Generally the theories we believe we call facts and the facts we disbelieve we call theories. Felix Cohen

"I had much rather you should impute to me great error of judgment than the smallest deviation from sincerity." President John Quincy Adams

"A people that values its privileges above its principles soon loses both. President Dwight D. Eisenhower

"Anyone who breaks one of the least of these commandments and teaches others to do the same will be called least in the Kingdom of Heaven, but whoever practices and teaches these commandments will be called great in the Kingdom of Heaven." Matthew 5:19

WALKING WITH THE WISE

All of us are influenced by others. Some of the others who influence us are wise while others are foolish. If we are more influenced by the wise, if we are walking with the wise, we are more likely to make wise decisions.

We read in 1 Kings, "God gave Solomon wisdom and very great insight, and a breadth of understanding as measureless as the sand on the seashore" (4:29). When we seek God, we learn in Proverbs 2:6, "For the Lord gives wisdom, from His mouth come knowledge and understanding" (KJV). In James 1:5 we discover "If any of you lacks wisdom, you should ask God, who gives generously to all without finding fault, and it will be given to him."

What can we learn from these Scriptures? 1. God will give wisdom to those who ask for it. 2. With wisdom comes knowledge and understanding. 3. God did this with King Solomon who used it to rule wisely.

Wisdom gives us the opportunity to see and to understand that which other men do not see and understand. Wisdom allows us to see relationships which exist, cause and effect and implications well into the future. Wisdom helps us to know God's will and to see what we should do on earth that would be in keeping with His will. Wisdom helps to see that true happiness is not in wealth or power.

But for God to give us this wisdom, we need to <u>talk</u> with God. That means prayer, earnest prayer. In that prayer we must demonstrate through thought and word that we are seeking to be close to God and that we truly want to do His will on earth. A person regarded as a genius, Albert Einstein, had the wisdom to say, "I want to know God's thoughts . . ., the rest are details."

Many of the wisest people who ever lived are still available to us through their written words. People with wisdom still living might be people near us or people we could seek out. We can learn from the wise but we must acknowledge that our ego might be in the way. The wise person knows that there is much wisdom to be gained by walking with the wise. Is there someone you need to walk with soon?

STUDY QUESTIONS

1. Identify three of the wisest people you have ever met. Why did you select these people?
2. Do you seek wisdom by first getting close to God and then asking for wisdom?
3. What wisdom, from you or from others, should you disseminate in order to make this a better world?

178

"A wise man talks because he has something to say. Fools talk because they have to say something." Anonymous

Proverbs 2:6-8: "For the Lord gives wisdom; from his mouth come knowledge and understanding. He holds success in store for the upright, he is a shield to those whose walk is blameless, for he guards the course of the just and protects the way of his faithful ones."

"Be careful whose approval you seek." Anonymous

DISCERNMENT

The word discern appears in the Bible at least 22 times including 12 times in Proverbs. The dictionary defines it as "the ability to see and understand people, things or situations clearly and intelligently." Church leader John MacArthur said, "discernment is nothing more than the ability to decide between truth and error, right and wrong." MacArthur continues "Discernment is the process of making careful distinctions in our thinking about truth." Discernment isn't just about our view of others. Psalm 19:12 says, "Who can discern his errors. Forgive my hidden faults." The context here is about being "pleasing in His sight." God also discerns us as in Psalm 139:3: "You discern my going out and my lying down."

Paul urges us to discern in Philippians 1:9: "And this is my prayer: that your love might abound more and more in knowledge and depth of insight, so that you might be able to discern what is best and may be pure and blameless until the day of Christ." We are told to discern what is best and follow that in our lives continuously. We are told that this discernment must come from the "Spirit of God." Without this Spirit of God man "does not accept the things that come from the Spirit of God" (1 Cor 2:14). Two references in 1 Kings talk of the "discerning heart." Solomon is speaking to God saying, "So give your servant a discerning heart to govern your people and to distinguish between right and wrong." (1 Kings 3:9) God's response to Solomon was recorded in 3:12 saying, "I will give you a wise and discerning heart." Note the relationship between wisdom and discernment. To distinguish between right and wrong, wisdom must be present.

Relate this to your own life. Wisdom and discernment are needed throughout the day as we make decisions. Knowing the difference between right and wrong is essential. Having the courage to always do what is right takes courage. But doing so will be pleasing to God.

STUDY QUESTIONS

1. Think about one of the tough decisions you have made in your life to date. To what extent was discernment present?
2. How can you help others around you to discover discernment and then practice it?
3. Think about a decision you will have to make in the future. How will you apply wisdom and discernment to your decision?

106A

"Wisdom will save you from the ways of wicked men, from men whose words are perverse." Proverbs 2:12

"All this I have told you so that you will not go astray." John 16:1

"Dear friends, do not believe every spirit, but test the spirits to see whether they are from God, because many false prophets have gone out into the world." 1 John 4:1

"Only those who dare to fail greatly can ever achieve greatly." Robert Kennedy

ACHIEVING HUMILITY

Before discussing how to achieve humility, let's define what we mean by humility. Jesus talked about humility in Mt 18:1-5 and Phil 2:3-4: "Do nothing out of selfish ambition or vain conceit. Rather, in humility value others above yourselves, not looking to your own interests but each of you to the interests of the others." In Mt 18 Jesus urged followers to practice humility. Humility as used in the New Testament (Mt 5) refers to not looking down on others (Mt 18 and Luke 14), gentleness, and not being overly concerned about prestige (Mt 18 and others). The New Testament says the humble shall be exalted and the proud will receive punishment.

Many people make the mistake in thinking that being humble means putting yourself down or thinking little of yourself. Instead, humility is a position of strength in which the person is sufficiently self confident to perform well while at the same time taking a position in which God is exalted above self. The proud have difficulty exalting God due to their pride. A humble person is more likely to help others and less likely to feel a need to promote self.

Dr. Harold Korver, President of Carolina College of Biblical Studies in Fayetteville, North Carolina, has a quote from Jamie Lash on his desk which reads, "Humility is not thinking less of yourself but thinking of yourself less." Consider what that means. It suggests that we can achieve humility by, first of all, thinking of ourselves less and thinking more about others. Be confident in who you are and the role you are playing in life unless God is directing you to other venues.

To achieve humility, stop to think about what is really important in life. First, think about our relationship to God. If we are willing to place him first and others second, that is a big step toward humility. A second step is to consider ways in which we might serve others. There are many people not far from us who need help. When we take time to help others, we are practicing humility by placing their needs above our own. A third step in achieving humility is to pray. In prayer we come before the Master to comment and to ask. It establishes a relationship in which God is #1 and we are #2 (or lower if others are involved).

What are you willing to do to achieve a greater level of humility in your life?

STUDY QUESTIONS

1. Do others describe you as a humble person, a person with humility?
2. What steps might you take to enhance your humility?
3. Describe a person you know who is known for humility.

133

"Whoever is happy will make others happy too. He who has courage and faith will never perish in misery." Anne Frank

"I count him braver who overcomes his desires than him who conquers his enemies; for the hardest victory is the victory over self." Aristotle (384-322 B C)

"I can't, I won't, I shouldn't, I will. For either good or evil." Anonymous

"Consider it pure joy, my brethren, whenever you face trials of many kinds, because you know that the testing of your faith develops perseverance." James 1:2-3

COURAGE TO BE WHO YOU ARE

Do you have the courage to be who you are? No one knows you better than you do. Not even your Mother or a spouse. You know your inner thoughts, your aspirations, your fears, what brings you joy and what you worry about. Yet most of us keep much of this to ourselves thinking that the rest of world would think some of these thoughts foolish, subject to ridicule or just not understandable. So we decide to be transparent to others revealing only selective parts of who we are. If you live your life in accordance with the teachings of the Bible and are in prayer with God daily, the person you really are needs to be known to others. We are told to be salt and light in the world (Matthew 5:13-16) and not "pepper and darkness" (Dan Pearson). Matthew goes on to say, "…let your light shine before others, that they may see your good deeds and glorify your Father in Heaven" (Matthew 5:16). What we can take from this passage is that our Christian life should not be hidden from the world. We should be glad in our faith and seek to extend it to others so that they are able to spend eternity in Heaven as well. While we are told to be as a "city built on a hill" (Matthew 5:14), we are also told to avoid being proud and boastful (Galatians 6:14).

There is a significant difference between being boastful and self-confident. A boastful person seeks to bring positive attention to self. A self-confident person is able to focus on ways in which he or she has the opportunity to serve God and others. As we grow in self-confidence, we might be willing to be more transparent (let others see who we really are) and thus mention to others some of our goals, thoughts, aspirations and fears. As we do this, we find it possible to pursue interests and abilities that have been latent up to that time. Gaining in self-confidence allows us to use the gifts given to us by God for His glory. Each of us should be encouraged to be the person God created us to be and to do those positive things for which we are gifted and have interest.

In order to do this, however, we need to be sure that we really do understand who we are. Sometimes we fool ourselves because of what others have said about us in the past. Or we might have had less than success at something we tried but we feel that if we tried again we could succeed. Abraham Lincoln had failure after failure early in his life. There is that fear of failure that keeps us from trying. A fear of failure can become a self-fulfilling prophecy. Too much fear of failure will ensure its realization. Overcoming that fear means taking some risk. When we reach the point when we see that the benefits that could come from taking a risk are greater in importance to us than the fear of failure, we are ready to move ahead with a fruitful and happy life that will be pleasing to God.

We all have to take risks. Sitting in a chair is a risk that the chair might collapse. At the same time, taking foolish risks are not encouraged by God or Godly people. One risk we should all take is to learn more about the person we are – what do we believe in, what do we value and what do we seek to accomplish. We need to know what brings us pleasure and what brings us peace. Taking personality and related tests can help us understand ourselves better. It can point out strengths that we thought might be there but now we have proof and, with the test results, it is also evident to others as well. It could be helpful to ask friends what they see as our greatest strengths. Observe how others respond to you and on what others compliment you as well as what brings smiles to others from what you say and do. Then build upon the positives.

One of your positives is likely in your inner thoughts. What do you spend time thinking about? Give some deep thought as to who you really are based on what you think about. Our inner thoughts could bubble to the surface in actions that we take. Compare these inner thoughts to the person you perceive that others think you are and how you currently see yourself. Courage is needed to push for narrowing the differences.

The purpose of discovering who you are is to unleash the potential within you and build the courage to be who you really are. None of us live to our potential. Overnight transformation is not likely so take it one step at a time without waiting long before taking the second step. Be driven by your goals and a strong self-concept and not by any negative or lukewarm reception from others. God will be pleased when you act on your gifts, your potential. Pleasing God, after all, should be our most important goal. What is the first step you need to take to become the person God would have you to be and you know you can become? Do you have the courage to take that first step? Once the goal is reached, you will be glad you took the needed action.

WISDOM AND COURAGE

Have you ever thought about how wisdom and courage make great partners? There are times in life when the paths we should take are not very well defined. There might be many unknowns yet a very important decision must be made and we lack the option of putting off the decision until the options become clearer. We should pray to God at those times for both wisdom and courage.

We need wisdom, first of all, to define the situation. Emotion, uncertainty and anxiety could cause us to poorly define what the situation is before us. If we fail to define the situation accurately, any decision we make will be the wrong decision. We need to pray and seek counsel to define the situation appropriately.

Once we have accurately defined what the situation is, we need wisdom to seek the choices we have relative to that decision. Again, prayer to God and seeking counsel from those who might see the situation clearly could be very helpful to us. But if it is our decision to make, we still must be able to see the options, understand the implications of the various choices and then have the wisdom to make the right decision..

Here is where courage fits into the partnership of wisdom and courage. There are times in life when we have concluded what the right decision is and when to make that decision. Yet we might lack the courage to make that decision. There is the uncertainty that it will turn out as well as we hope it will. There is the criticism from others that we might think is certain to come. There is the possible risk of money and reputation. The human tendency is for people to react to a decision initially on the basis of how it will affect them instead of the greater good. Yet your decision is about the greater good. Courage is required to make the right decision, to make it at the right time and to deliver it in a manner that focuses on the decision rather than self and without anger or other emotions that might cause others to misunderstand the situation.

Courage includes willingness to consider what the Scripture tells us. Proverbs 1:5 reads: "...let the wise listen and add to their learning, and let the discerning get guidance..." Courage is best done with wisdom and wisdom requires our courage.

The next time you face an important decision, will you have both the wisdom to define the situation and its options and then the courage to make the right decision, at the right time and in the right manner?

STUDY QUESTIONS

1. Think of a situation with similarities to what is described above. How did you define the issue, the big question on which a decision must be made?
2. How did it turn out?
3. How did you involve God through prayer in this situation? 73

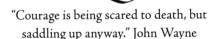

"Courage is being scared to death, but saddling up anyway." John Wayne

"Tough times never last, tough people do." James W. Jones

Garrison Keillor: When in doubt, look intelligent.

Romans 12:2: "Do not conform to the pattern of this world, but be transformed by the renewing of your mind. Then you will be able to test and approve what God's will is – his good, pleasing and perfect will."

UNDAUNTED COURAGE

Stephen E. Ambrose, well known for his biographies of Dwight Eisenhower and Richard Nixon, wrote the book, *Undaunted Courage*. In this New York Times Bestseller, he describes the courage initially of Thomas Jefferson and then Meriwether Lewis and William Clark. Jefferson had attempted earlier to send explorers to find a land route to the Pacific Ocean but without success. Once the Louisiana Purchase was completed in 1803, the United States had legal right to property of which the boundaries were unclear. What was in this territory was largely unknown except for the lower parts of the Missouri River and previous contact with Indians in what is now South Dakota.

Thomas Jefferson became the United States President in 1801 and thus gained the rights of that position to make an expedition possible with the support of the government. The British previously had some success in exploring western Canada thus motivating Jefferson to initiate an expedition to thwart the efforts of the British who Jefferson thought might come down into what is now Oregon. Meriwether Lewis became the Secretary to Jefferson and lived in what later became known as the White House. Lewis was a natural choice to lead the expedition. By nature a wanderer, he enjoyed travel where wild animals, sources of water and food were unpredictable and encounters with Indians were likely.

In the first year, Lewis gathered supplies with support of the Army (Lewis was made a Captain) and individuals (a contractor made a keel boat). William Clark joined him and they set out with a group going up the Missouri River. After a winter encampment, they set out into unknown territory keeping a log of flora and fauna as well as rivers and streams as they went. Eventually they reached the Columbia River and came to the Pacific Ocean.

Undaunted Courage is the title and theme of the book. In spite of the enormous task of entering unknown territory with scant supplies (only what they could carry), their courage was undaunted. Now take a look at your courage level. Courage is impacted by knowledge, experience, curiosity, motivation, personal and general attitude toward the possibilities and worthiness of the goal. How well do those factors impact you as you look at what is in front of you each day, week and year?

The product of undaunted courage can be success. Lewis and Clark were successful in reaching the Pacific Ocean by building pieces of success during the expedition as they recorded new knowledge and perceptions to be given to President Jefferson. They had success each day that they stayed alive. Each of us can have "undaunted courage" each day as we build on our successes and work with courage toward accomplishment of an ultimate set of goals. But like Paul in the New Testament, we must have perseverance in that courage even when the situation is discouraging and we are tempted to turn back. Paul, in Philippians 3:13-14 said: "Brothers and sisters, I do not consider myself yet to have taken hold of it. But one thing I do: Forgetting what is behind and straining toward what is ahead, I press on toward the goal to win the prize for which God has called me heavenward in Christ Jesus."

What is the level of your "undaunted courage"? Will it take you to completion of your goals? Are your goals sufficiently clear? For Lewis and Clark the goals were very clear. How much do you want the goals to be reached? Do you have "undaunted courage"?

STUDY QUESTIONS

1. Describe for yourself the relationship between your goals in life and the level of your courage to attain them.
2. What is the level of motivation with your goals? Are you determined to make them happen regardless of the courage it takes or do you look at your goals as events that would be nice if they were to happen?
3. Who is the most courageous person you know? Describe an act of courage on his or her part.

342

PERSEVERANCE

How strong is your perseverance? James 1 describes perseverance in our lives. James talks about perseverance as a goal in and of itself. James 1:2-4 tells us to "Consider it pure joy, my brothers, whenever you face trials of many kinds, because you know that the testing of your faith produces perseverance." James continues, "Perseverance must finish its work so that you may be mature and complete, not lacking anything." While "trials of many kinds" produce perseverance through "testing of your faith," the result is achieving maturity and completeness. A sign in a restaurant recently said, "You miss 100% of the shots you don't take." Each time we face a challenge, we can refuse to take the shot or we can persevere forward. Only through perseverance do we accomplish our goals and, as James describes it, reach maturity and completeness.

The writer of Hebrews 12:1 tells us to throw off that which hinders us and the sin that entangles us so that we might "run with perseverance the race marked out for us." That race is to follow Jesus. To run with perseverance means to run without letting things or people get in our way or to give up for any reason. In Romans 5:2-4, Paul tells us that we should "rejoice in the hope of the glory of God" and "we also rejoice in our sufferings, because we know that suffering produces perseverance; perseverance, character; and character, hope." Perseverance will contribute toward building character that embodies all that is good about us. Character is built during a lifetime and perseverance allows us to continually build character. To the extent to which our character is strong, we will withstand the temptations of this life and remain (persevere) true to God. To persevere means that our character does not change daily or according to the direction of those around us who do not share our faith. We are not persuaded to follow paths that take us away from our faith and that tears down our character. We persevere in the path of righteousness, in the path of Christian faith.

Perseverance is significant in our prayers. We are told to "pray without ceasing" (1 Thes 5:17 KJV). In other words, we are told to pray with perseverance. James 1:6 adds, "But when you ask, you must believe and not doubt, because the one who doubts is like a wave of the sea, blown and tossed by the wind." When we persevere in our faith or in other parts of our lives, we do not change as the wind changes but rather remain steadfast in what we have set out to do, steadfast in what we believe, keeping our goal in sight. Our goal is to demonstrate our Christian faith in all that we do, think and say. We should do that which pleases God.

STUDY QUESTIONS

1. Describe a situation in which perseverance paid off for you.
2. What is there in your life that you would describe as persevering?
3. What are the things that can tempt you to deter from your perseverance?

285

Blessed is the one who perseveres under trial because, having stood the test, that person will receive the crown of life that the Lord has promised to those who love him. When tempted, no one should say, 'God is tempting me.' For God cannot be tempted by evil, nor does he tempt anyone; but each person is tempted when they are dragged away by their own evil desire and enticed. Then, after desire has conceived, it gives birth to sin; and sin, when it is full-grown, gives birth to death. James 1:12-15

"You can fake virtue for an audience. You can't fake it in your own eyes." Ayn Rand

"It's really hard to take back stupid." Dr. Phil

VIRTUE AND TOLERATION

Let's talk about virtues (our principles) and their relationship to toleration. Helen Keller is quoted as saying that "toleration . . . is the greatest gift of the mind; it requires the same effort of the brain that it takes to balance oneself on a bicycle." The limitation of that statement without qualifiers is that it was toleration that brought Adolf Hitler to power in Germany in 1933. Once Hitler was in power he sought more power, first in Germany, and then in the surrounding countries and eventually power over the world. Hitler was himself very intolerant of others not like himself and promoted intolerance with the German people building upon years of prejudice that existed, not only of Jews, but also of any other people not like himself. Germany expressed intolerance for much of humanity.

Toleration is a virtue only when it allows others to be themselves and thus reach their positive potential within the laws of God and man. The Allied Forces (1939-45) fought the intolerance of Germany. Tolerance is not a virtue when it fosters intolerance. Tolerance in its extreme case allows others to do anything they want to do, whenever they want to do it and by whatever means. The English word for this is chaos. Jesus was tolerant of a wide range of people but he was intolerant of the Pharisees because they added rules and regulations that went beyond the actual precepts of the Old Testament Scriptures.

So what must go with tolerance to make it a virtue? He who stands for nothing stands, in effect, for anything desired by others. We cannot be tolerant when we see another person breaking the law. We cannot let a murderer go free because we need to be tolerant of his or her desire to kill someone. So, first of all, <u>we must recognize that toleration must have its limits.</u> Toleration, like freedom, is not an absolute. Freedom and toleration have limits when exercised to limit the freedom of others.

But where do the limits come from? What one person holds as a virtue, such as Hitler's belief that he represented the superior race, <u>ceases to be a virtue when it begins to infringe on the virtues and rights of others</u>. The right to life is a virtue most of us recognize. We must stop the murderer even though we are being intolerant of the would-be murderer's values and desires. The

Bible is our best guide to virtue or qualities acceptable to God. We hear the virtues recorded in the Bible advocated by people we admire and trust. Each of us must discover the virtues, our principles, by which we will live. One of these virtues should be toleration of diversity in society by which we benefit from others being different from us as long as they in turn respect our right to our virtues. <u>Toleration of diversity as a virtue encourages us to be tolerant, even encourage, different viewpoints and perspectives which can contribute toward making this a better world</u>. However, this toleration must not extend beyond what we have been taught in the Bible as the appropriate virtues or principles by which God commands us to live. Read Psalm 1:1-6. By knowing our virtues, we learn when to be tolerant of others and when we must resist the intolerant actions of others.

STUDY QUESTIONS

1. Think about what virtues you hold dear. What are the principles by which you guide your behavior every day?
2. Is one of those virtues toleration for others to have a right to express their opinion even when it differs from yours?
3. Where is it appropriate for you to be tolerant and when should you be intolerant (when it violates your virtues)?

205B

AUTHORITY AND RESPONSIBILITY

Every organization and every person must work to balance these two in order to be good at whatever is to be or intended to be. A large corporation, a small business, a church, a government and even a family must recognize that <u>authority must equal responsibility</u>. When authority is exercised without responsibility you have a dictatorship or an unfit parent. When responsibility is assumed without authority you have disappointment and frustration at best. The greater the authority, the greater is our responsibility for both action and inaction.

So what is authority? Authority is the power to do something whether it is said, a physical act or influence. Authority can be earned through accomplishment, given through a position (president of a company or mother of a family) and authority can come from influence (such as a speaker or performer who exerts authority through what they do and their role model). Every one of us has some authority, therefore, every one of us has responsibility to meet. Each of us has authority over how we will act, how we will think, what we will say and what we will do. It might be argued that we have no control over what we do at work but we must remember that we made the decision to work in that position initially.

Responsibility is accepting the fact that our exercise of authority has effects, has consequences, both good and bad. We are responsible for those effects, those consequences. Responsibility means that we accept that we are liable for what happens to people and what people do as a result of our actions, both good and bad. If we don't like those results, then we need to accept the responsibility for changing the effect we are having.

It is tempting, and sometimes easy, to blame others for the results that happen rather than to accept responsibility. There are times when others <u>are</u> to blame, that <u>they</u> are responsible. But blaming others is too easy for escaping responsibility. If you sin, don't blame your preacher.

If we want to lead in our job, our church or our family, we must recognize that the justification for our leading is not our ego; it is the intended effect of our leading. The intended effect is what we are seeking to create. On a baseball team the person who hits in the winning run is only partly responsible for winning the game. Accepting responsibility can be very positive as we are given the credit for a positive result. Seek positive results, use what authority you have to make it happen and then accept the praise or the blame for the outcome. The great people in history are people who sought authority and then used it for positive results. You are urged to seek authority within your set of abilities and talents and then use that authority to make this a better world. Not everyone will praise you for what you consider to be a positive act, but the intended effect is not the praise but making this a better world and pleasing God. Sometimes, in creating a better world we have critics. Sometimes our intended effect misses the mark. Disappointment, along with praise, is part of accepting responsibility. However, to make this a better world, everyone should accept responsibility for <u>his or her</u> exercise of authority. Use the authority you have or are given to lead toward positive results that will bring honor and glory to God. Then you are responsible for at least your part in the outcome whether praise, criticism or some of both.

It is good for us to remember the Biblical principle that Paul puts forward in Galatians 6:7-9: "Do not be deceived: God cannot be mocked. A man reaps what he sows. Whoever sows to please their flesh, from the flesh will reap destruction; whoever sows to please the Spirit, from the Spirit will reap eternal life. Let us not become weary in doing good, for at the proper time we will reap a harvest if we do not give up."

STUDY QUESTIONS

1. What authority do you think that you have in your family, church, work and other places?
2. How are you doing on accepting responsibility for your use of authority?
3. What changes in either your use of authority or accepting responsibility are appropriate in your life?

65A

ARROGANCE

Few people are willing to admit that they are arrogant, yet most of us are arrogant at times. Being arrogant means being self-centered, oblivious to the needs and rights of others and willing to assert yourself regardless of the feelings of others. Note that God condemns arrogance in Proverbs 8:13: "To fear the Lord is to hate evil; I hate pride and arrogance, evil behavior and perverse speech."

Each of us needs to be self confident in what we do and in being the person we are. Yet self-confidence allows us to reach out to others, to be sympathetic, to be concerned, to want to help others as we get beyond our own needs and wants. Arrogance can, in fact, come from a person who lacks self-confidence and is seeking that confidence by putting down others in order to elevate self. Have you ever met an arrogant person who was truly happy inside, happy with being the person he or she is? Being arrogant presupposes an attitude toward others that holds others as being lesser persons than self. This negative view of others will lead to personal unhappiness.

When we encounter an arrogant person, we tend to shy away from them and they see our distance as proof of their inferiority. An arrogant person rarely has an accurate view of self and is likely to blame others for any shortfall from the ideal without assuming any responsibility.

What can we do? We can pray for the individual. We can befriend the person thus lifting them up and giving them confidence without arrogance. The arrogant person might not accept our efforts but we will have made the effort to help. We can stand up to the individual, not by being arrogant ourselves, but refusing to allow ourselves to be put down. Be self-confident in the face of arrogance. But remember that God loves everyone.

STUDY QUESTIONS

1. Are you ever arrogant? What circumstances might cause this trait to arise in you?

2. What has worked for you in dealing with arrogant people?
3. Have you ever prayed for an arrogant person? Have you been able to help that person?

72

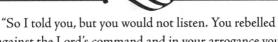

"So I told you, but you would not listen. You rebelled against the Lord's command and in your arrogance you marched up into the hill country" Deuteronomy 1:43

"To fear the Lord is to hate evil; I hate pride and arrogance, evil behavior and perverse speech" Proverbs 8:13

"A person's wisdom yields patience; it is to one's glory to overlook an offense."

PRIDE

All of us should have some pride in who we are. However, pride in excess can be our downfall. C. S. Lewis wrote in his journal about pride. An abridged version of what he said about pride is as follows:

> According to Christian teachers, the essential vice, the utmost evil, is Pride. Unchastity, anger, greed, drunkenness, and all that, are mere fleabites in comparison: It was through Pride that the devil became the devil. Pride leads to every other vice; it is the complete anti-God state of mind. . . . . If you want to find out how proud you are the easiest way is to ask yourself, 'How much do I dislike it when other people snub me, or refuse to take any notice of me? The point is that every person's pride is in competition with everyone else's pride. It is because I wanted to be the big noise at the party that I am so annoyed at someone else being the big noise. Now what you want to get clear is that Pride is *essentially* competitive – is competitive by its very nature – while the other vices are competitive only, so to speak, by accident. Pride gets no pleasure out of having something, only having more of it than the next man. We say that people are proud of being rich, or clever, or good-looking, but they are not. They are proud of being richer, or cleverer, or better-looking than others. If everyone else became equally rich, or clever, or good-looking there would be nothing to be proud about. It is the comparison that makes you proud; the pleasure of being above the rest. Once the element of competition has gone, pride has gone. That is why I say that Pride is essentially competitive in a way that the other vices are not.

This is a statement from the journal of C. S. Lewis. As you listen to what C. S. Lewis said about pride, you might be thinking, do you mean I shouldn't have any pride in who I am? Like most things in life, we must achieve a <u>balance</u> in our pride. We all need to have sufficient pride to have self-respect, self-confidence. A level of self-respect is required in order to function in society. Courage to act is based on an appropriate level of pride. However, the pride C. S. Lewis talks about is one in which we are very proud in comparison to others, a pride that comes only when we can find a person who has less of something than we do. This is a pride that causes us to say and do things that are arrogant and offensive to others. When we are arrogant or offensive, others tend to withdraw from contact with us making it more difficult for us to do our best and succeed in our relationships with others. Pride can make us self-centered rather than other person centered. Jesus focused on other people rather than self yet had the ability, a sufficient level of self-confidence, to become the person who has had more effect on others than any other person who has lived.

Pride can be dangerous. For this reason, the Apostle Peter admonished Christians in I Peter 5:6: "...humble ourselves under the mighty hand of God, that He may exalt you at the proper time." Each of us needs to find that appropriate level of pride. Consider that excess pride can destroy our ability to witness to others about our Christian faith. Think about how pride is a driving force for you. Are you proud of your being "above the rest?" Or is your pride at an appropriate balance?

From C S Lewis, The Beloved Works of C S Lewis, p. (1984), p. 346

STUDY QUESTIONS

1. When does pride become a problem? Think of the response for yourself and then think of the response for other people you know.
2. What is the most important point made by C. S. Lewis in the above quote in your estimation?
3. If your pride is a problem for you, what do you plan to do about it? Remember, those with excessive pride are not likely to want to admit having it.

93A

BEING OTHER-PERSON CENTERED

Everyone has personal needs that must be addressed. We need food and shelter. We have emotional and physical needs (not just wants) to be met in order to serve others. Once we have taken care of these basic needs, we then are able to think about the other people in the world. However, if we do not take care of ourselves, we are in no position to help anyone else.

Taking care of our own needs, however, doesn't take all of our time. The rest of our time could be devoted to going beyond our needs to satisfying our wants. Or it could be a combination of pursuing some wants and devoting the remainder of our available time to meeting the needs of others. To do this, we must be other-person centered.

What does that mean? It means that beyond your basic needs, our focus in life is not on self but on others. Mother Teresa is a fine example of a person who was other-person centered. Her basic needs were met even though she defined those needs in a very minimal way. That allowed her ample time to pursue her passion, being other-person centered.

What happens when we are other-person centered? We do more than talk about the needs of others and how others or the government should help the needy. Our behavior focuses on what the needs of others are and how we can go about helping them meet that need. Those needs go beyond food, water, shelter and health. It goes to emotional needs. It extends to making this a better day for someone by a kind deed that you were not required or expected to do. Being other-person centered means thinking of how you can make the life of others more pleasant.

Let us finally take note of the words of Scripture in Philippians 2:3 -4: "Do nothing out of selfish ambition or vain conceit. Rather, in humility, value others above yourselves, not looking to our own interests but each of you to the interests of the others." What are you willing to do today to make the lives of others more enjoyable? Are you other-person centered?

STUDY QUESTIONS

1. Think of how you spent your day yesterday. How much of it was spent in meeting your needs and wants and how much of it was devoted to being other-person centered?
2. Among the people you meet in a seven-day cycle, who do you think of as being a person you could help by a physical act or a kind word?
3. Who is the most other-person centered individual you know? What does this person do?

50

How to lead a moral life: "Use for yourself little,
but give to others much." Albert Einstein

"It is our attitude at the beginning of a difficult
task which, more than anything else, will affect its
successful outcome." Psychologist William James

"Humor is the solvent against the abrasiveness of
life." Senator Alan Simpson (Wyoming) at the
funeral of President George H. W. Bush

"The fear of the Lord is the beginning
of wisdom." Psalm 111:10

"The man who does more than he is paid for will soon
be paid for more than he does." Napoleon Hill

COMPASSION

Let's think about what compassion means. Compassion is the deep caring for others which can lead to action on our part in which we demonstrate that our concern for others is more than words but rather action that will make a difference in the lives of others. Psalm 103:13 reads:

> As a father has compassion on his children, so the Lord
> has compassion on those who fear Him.

In Matthew 9:36 Jesus had compassion on the crowd, "because they were harassed and helpless, like sheep without a shepherd." We should all work to be like Jesus and thus show compassion. The New Testament records many instances in which Jesus showed compassion for people. In one case the Bible records that Jesus wept due to his concern for others. Psalm 145:8-9 states: "The Lord is gracious and compassionate, slow to anger and rich in love. The Lord is good to all; he has compassion on all He has made." We should attempt to be no less. To make his point in parables Jesus used compassion as in the case of the prodigal son when "his father saw him and was filled with compassion for him" (Luke 15:20).

Most of us are in need of compassion at times in our lives but there are some who are in such a state that a perpetual display of compassion is appropriate. We appreciate it when others show compassion for us in a time of sorrow. As a result, we know that others will also appreciate compassion being shown for them in their time of need. We are told to do for others what we would have them do for us.

When we consider the nature of compassion, we see that it is a form of love. Love means caring about another person. The Apostle John quotes Jesus as saying, "A new command I give you: Love one another. As I have loved you, so you must love one another" (John 13:34). When we love a person, showing compassion for them is a natural thing to do. That which is natural should never be difficult to do. As a result, showing compassion for any person, whether we know them or not, should be a natural thing to do for any Christian.

Think back to when others have demonstrated compassion to you. How did you feel as a result? Think of instances in which you have demonstrated compassion toward others in the past. Be of a mind to find opportunities to show compassion in the days to come. You will feel good that you took Christlike action.

STUDY QUESTIONS

1. Think of three times when you have shown compassion for another person or group in the past. Did someone have to urge you to do this or was it something that came naturally to you?
2. Are you able to think of a situation in which you might go out today to demonstrate compassion as Jesus would? Will you do it?
3. Think of a time when compassion was shown to you. How did you feel about it?

279

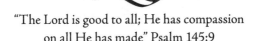

"The Lord is good to all; He has compassion on all He has made" Psalm 145:9

"The worst of all deceptions is self-deception." Plato (427-347 B C)

WISDOM AND CONFIDENCE

Wisdom and confidence. What a powerful combination. This is the third in the series on wisdom. First, the topic of wisdom was introduced and then the relationship between wisdom and courage. Wisdom and confidence are closely related.

First we need wisdom to define any situation. Without a wisdom-guided *analysis of the scenario*, confidence can lead us to the wrong action. Wisdom also tells us *how to address a situation*. Wisdom can come from experience and from preparation (formal or informal) for the event. *Timing* is a third element of wisdom. The right decision at the wrong time is often a wrong decision. The fourth element of wisdom is in *knowing how* to accomplish the action. An abrasive, insensitive approach in applying a wise decision is not likely to carry the day.

But there must also be confidence in order to apply wisdom. Philippians 4:13 records Paul saying, "I can do all things through Him who gives me strength." We all have some confidence. Some of us like to have others think we have more confidence than we actually have. We vary in our confidence to some extent based on a situation. There are times when we need a lot of confidence. Confidence is closely related to courage because courage can give us the needed confidence. Faith can also give us confidence. When faith and courage are combined, confidence can often rise to the level required by the circumstances. When we sense a lack of confidence we are not likely to push our agenda to the fullest. When we lack confidence in accomplishing something, others will sense this and will tend to discount our action. Combined, this lack of confidence could doom the plan.

If the plan is wise (as tested with others and revelation from God) and you have the courage to accomplish the plan, how do you gain the needed confidence? Three strategies include: Talking with others who will encourage you, having others in whom you have confidence and they have experience in the anticipated action and, most importantly, prayer asking God to guide you. Use all three.

The biggest challenge might be in combining wisdom with courage and confidence. If unbounded courage and confidence leads us away from wisdom, the outcome will not be good. There must be a balance within the three for the right outcome. Which comes first? Start with prayer seeking wisdom to carefully define the situation. Look at Scriptures about wisdom and confidence. Confidence without wisdom is a certain disaster. But wisdom alone does not create the desired action. Let wisdom find the right action and then apply confidence to make it happen. The result can be a better world, one pleasing to God.

STUDY QUESTIONS

1. Think about your attitude toward yourself. Do you see yourself as capable of making a positive difference in this world? Can you make a positive difference in your work place?
2. What are your gifts and talents? Your education and experience? Do you work in areas that have a high correlation to your gifts, talents, education and experience?
3. In the film "Bridge Over the River Kwai" the workers were told, "Be happy in your work." But they weren't. What does it take to be happy in your work? When it is present, what happens to your attitude toward the work?

221

LOVE AND OUR PERSONAL PREFERENCES

Let's talk about expressing love and its relationship to our personal preferences. The Apostle John recorded that Jesus told His followers that they "must love one another" (John 13:34). We are told by the Apostle Paul that, of our attributes, love is the greatest (I Corinthians 13:13). But some people are not lovely by most human standards and even more do not fit within our personal preferences. We might witness behavior we think is despicable. We might hear language that makes us cringe. We might see people who we prefer to avoid. So how do we as Christians deal with this dilemma of loving the unlovely?

One alternative is to follow our preferences and not worry about how it is inconsistent with our profession of Christian faith. This displeases God and is a poor witness of our faith. We could be seen as a hypocrite. We state one thing in our faith confession and then act in ways that Jesus Christ told us to avoid. This means we have sinned. Not a good option.

Another option would be to examine which of our personal preferences might be inconsistent with our Christian faith. Most of our preferences will likely be consistent with our faith but there are likely to be some that are clearly inconsistent with our faith. The big challenge we have is that once we identify those personal preferences that are inconsistent with our faith, to make the tough decision of whether we will follow our faith or the preferences that are inconsistent with our faith. We should pray to God for help in this process.

Because God has uniquely created each of us, we will have preferences. There are many strong, positive preferences that need to continue to guide our lives. But what preferences do we have that are based on animosity, hatred, jealousy, pride, anger, people being different than we are or just being uncomfortable due to a new situation? Our guide should not be the intensity of our anger, pride or another negative driving force, but instead let our preferences and our actions be guided by "agape" (Godly) love, the kind of love the Apostle John describes. We are told to love our enemies. If we do that, how can we avoid loving every person we encounter? And if "agape" love governs our relationships with others, no personal preference can stand in the way. How does "agape" love determine <u>your</u> relationships with others?

STUDY QUESTIONS

1. What are some of your personal preferences that could conflict with your Christian faith?
2. Take one such preference and consider in detail how it conflicts with your Christian faith. Think about what your dilemma is.
3. To what extent does agape love govern who you are?

246

"You, dear children, are from God and have overcome
the, because the one who is in you is greater than
the one who is in the world" 1 John 4:4

"Grace be with you, mercy, and peace, from God
the Father, and from the Lord Jesus Christ, the
Son of the Father, in truth and love" 2 John 3

"When the door of happiness closes, another opens; but
often we look so long at the closed door that we do not
see the one which has opened for us." Helen Keller

TIME AND MONEY

David B. Norris once commented, "How you spend your time is more important than how you spend your money. Money mistakes can be corrected, but time is gone forever." Someone once said that we can tell what is important about a person by looking at their appointment book and his or her checkbook and credit card statement. *It tells how the person has spent these precious commodities.* How you spend these two things, time and money, demonstrates what kind of person you are.

Good use of time requires allotments to taking care of ourselves (food, rest, health), honorable work (contributing to the economy while earning a living to pay our own expenses), time for God and others (helping other people either individually or through a group like a service club or our church as well as worship of God) and finally, having some moments to ourselves to collect our thoughts, to pursue gifts God has given us or enjoy the earth's beauty.

Our resources of time and money should wisely be utilized to help us reach our goals. Without goals, we are like to use these resources in random ways without working together. Our resources should also be utilized in parallel with our other values. We achieve much of what we want in life if we can coordinate our resources along with our gifts to accomplish what is really important. Both time and money should be utilized in ways that are consistent with our Christian faith.

Good use of money has a strong parallel to the use of time. Both need to be used to take care of ourselves without being overly indulgent, to care for others and for our commitment to God while pursuing our gifts and interests for a life pleasing to God. Taking appropriate care of time and money is a matter of stewardship. The Bible in Luke 16:10 exhorts us through the words of Jesus: "Whoever can be trusted with very little can also be trusted with much, and whoever is dishonest with very little will also be dishonest with much." How well are you doing in allotting your time and money to the appropriate things in the appropriate amounts at the right time?

STUDY QUESTIONS

1. When you look at how you have spent your time and your money over the past seven days, what does that say about what is really important to you?
2. To what extent do you plan out your use of time to ensure that time is spent on that which is most important?
3. To what extent are you aware of where your money goes?

61

"For the love of money is a root of all kinds of evil. Some people, eager for money, have wandered from the faith and pierced themselves with many griefs" 1 Timothy 6:10

"Two people owed money to a certain moneylender. One owed him five hundred denari, and the other fifty. Neither of them had the money to pay him back, so he forgave the debts of both. Now which of them will love him more?" Luke 7:41-42

BEING ARTICULATE

Everyone talks but much of the time we are not articulate. To be articulate, one must have a clear line between the idea in the brain and the words that clearly communicate that idea in a fashion that causes the recipient to fully understand the thought. Psalm 45:1 encourages us to be articulate. It reads, "My heart is stirred by a noble theme as I recite my verses for the king; my tongue is the pen of a skillful writer." In a real sense, there is always some corruption of the ideal communication. There are several ways in which the idea fails to be articulately communicated.

One is that the idea is not clearly formed in the brain of the person wanting to communicate the thought. We must clearly know what we want to communicate before there can be any hope of any person understanding it. We need to think through an idea before it starts coming out of our mouth or communicated in writing. Concentrating on what we <u>want to say</u> is not enough. We must concentrate as precisely as possible on what it is that we want to <u>communicate</u>.

A second problem in being articulate is the choice of words to communicate the thought from the brain. Often the words are poorly chosen or vague so that the original thought is already blurred. When the thought is clear and time is taken to calmly communicate, a careful choice of words will articulately communicate the idea.

A third problem in being articulate is interference including noise, other people talking or other activities taking place in the vicinity. Any of these can make it hard to hear what is said or hard to concentrate thus garbling the intended message.

A fourth problem in being articulate is with the intended recipient. If that person is not listening intently or has prejudged the communication, this can cause only what they expect to hear to be received rather what is said. Inattentive listeners and readers will speculate on the meaning and thus form conclusions that are not in line with the message.

Being articulate is often confused with being a good entertainer. President John F. Kennedy was articulate while President Ronald Reagan was a good entertainer even though the media often called him a great communicator. A good entertainer pleases the audience and keeps their attention with humor and light conversation. An articulate speaker or writer has something of some importance to say that is clearly understood by the recipients.

Why should we be articulate? The best result from a communication is more likely when the message is clearly understood. We lose much of the value of the original thought when we are unable to articulately send the message or fail to ascertain the meaning of a message we have received. How might **you** become more articulate?

STUDY QUESTIONS

1. Rate yourself on how articulate you are in communicating with others. Are you more articulate when speaking or writing?
2. What steps could you take to become more articulate?
3. What are the differences between an entertaining speaker and an articulate speaker? How many times have you heard a speaker who was both?

81A

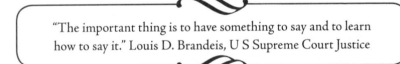

"The important thing is to have something to say and to learn how to say it." Louis D. Brandeis, U S Supreme Court Justice

CONVICTION OVER COMPROMISE

Think about the relationship between conviction and compromise. Historian John Patrick Diggins described John Quincy Adams, our sixth President, as one who "favored conviction over compromise and preferred discipline to convenience. A rare President."

John Quincy Adams, like his father, John Adams, our second President, was indeed a rare man. He spoke seven languages and had lived in those cultures. He had been Secretary of State before becoming the President. He was a man of conviction and was clear about where he stood on the issues of his day. He was also a man who disciplined himself to do what he thought to be the right thing rather than what was convenient or what others urged him to do.

How well would that describe you or even other people you know? Being a person of conviction means making decisions about personal, social and major issues of the day. A person without convictions is a person who is easily won over to any issue. Gullible is one word for this. When we lack convictions we are easily influenced and will change to side with whomever we are with at the moment.

Having a Christian faith is an important conviction. In Revelation 3:15-16, John talked about luke warm Christians whose conviction about their faith was not strong. Jesus taught us to be strong in our faith, to withstand temptations and to tell the world about our faith. That requires a strong conviction.

At the same time, having a strong conviction about every issue is not a virtue unless we have learned the various sides of each issue and have carefully and fairly considered the options before reaching a conclusion. Have you ever been accused of sometimes being wrong in your convictions but never in doubt? Most of us have convictions in areas of personal knowledge and experience but are without convictions in areas where we are still learning and have limited or no experience.

The second part of the historian's comment about John Quincy Adams was that he preferred discipline over convenience. We'll talk about that in another program. In the meantime, think about what your convictions are and whether they are sound convictions based on fact or random thoughts based on bias and lack of knowledge. If based on rational thought and facts, stand your ground (Ephesians 6:10-20) when your ground is solid. Don't compromise when your convictions are solidly based or based on your Christian faith.

STUDY QUESTIONS

1. In what areas do you have knowledge and/or experience to cause you to have sound convictions?
2. In what areas of knowledge or experience are you interested in getting to the point where you might have convictions?
3. Is your Christian faith one of your convictions? 191

"Happy is the man who findeth wisdom, and the man who getteth understanding." Proverbs 3:13 KJV

"Love must be sincere. Hate what is evil; cling to what is good. Be devoted to one another in brotherly love. Honor one another above yourselves. Never be lacking in zeal, but keep your spiritual fervor, serving the Lord. Be joyful in hope, patient in affliction, faithful in prayer. Share with God's people who are in need. Practice hospitality." Romans 12:9-13

"A religious mind is ever looking out of itself, is ever pondering God's words, is ever looking into them with the angels, is ever realizing to Him on whom it depends, and who is the centre of all truth and good." Cardinal John Henry Newman

DISCIPLINE OVER CONVENIENCE

Historian John Patrick Diggins described John Quincy Adams, our sixth President, as "He favored conviction over compromise and preferred discipline to convenience. A rare President." In the previous program, we talked about conviction over compromise. Now let's explore discipline over convenience.

The term discipline as used in this context refers to having goals and standards to which a person is steadfastly committed. Discipline is the process by which a person steadfastly stays with a project or commitment in spite of forces working against that commitment. Hebrews 12:6 says, "the Lord disciplines the one he loves." We discipline ourselves when we keep our focus, don't go down rabbit trails or otherwise fail to do what we set out to do. A person who competes in the Olympics is a person who must have considerable discipline in order to keep the mind and energy focused on doing the best in order to win the gold medal.

Convenience, on the other hand, is about taking the path that requires the least work and the greatest short-term benefits. Some issues can be decided by convenience such as when looking for a place to sit down. The first available chair might be convenient. There was no principle involved and no principle or ethical issue involved. We need discipline in those things that make a difference even though it might seem small or inconvenient. Hebrews 12:11 tells us, "No discipline seems pleasant at the time..." but later on "it produces a harvest of righteousness and peace for those who have been trained by it."

A person with no goals has no need for discipline. There is nothing to discipline self to do as part of attaining a goal. But people without goals have only accidental success in life and are seldom happy. God gives each of us at least one gift and we can be happy as we set goals related to our gifts and then discipline ourselves to attain those goals. Discipline is putting the muscle in motivation. Motivation can be weak, strong or somewhere in between. Strong motivation (I really want to do this) joined with discipline (I must do this) results in accomplishment.

John Quincy Adams was a person with goals and the will to discipline himself in order to come as close to attaining those goals as possible. He would choose convenience only when it had no impact on his goals. In the last hour, what have you decided on the basis of convenience and what have you disciplined yourself to do? What are your goals in life and how will you discipline yourself to attain them?

STUDY QUESTIONS

1. In what parts of your life do you exercise self-discipline today?
2. Are there areas of your life in which you know that you should exercise discipline but have not yet done so? Think about some goals on which you have made little progress.
3. Who is the most disciplined person you know? What do they do? 192

"We're not wise because we have God's word. We're not wise because we desire God's word. We're not even wise because we read God's word. We're wise only when we keep and obey God's word." Pastor Dr. David Jeremiah

"I have no greater joy than to hear that my children are walking in the truth." 3 John: 4

"Do not put the Lord your God to the test." Matthew 4:7

DISCIPLINED PEOPLE

All of us are disciplined to some extent. We get up for our day and we do some things during the day. But disciplined people are those who not only have a plan for the day but also then discipline themselves to follow the plan. What does being disciplined require? There must be adequate health to allow us to have control over our own behavior. There must also be some goals, a plan at least in a general sense, about what needs to happen today and this week. This plan must indicate the talent and physical ability needed prior to applying discipline. Discipline is the force within us that keeps us at the task(s) (plan) before us whether they were set by others or by us. It goes beyond motivation.

As we read the life of Jesus Christ in the four gospels, we hear about why He came (Luke 2:34-35, 4:18-19) and what He plans to do at that point in time. We do not see Jesus asking the apostles, what do you think we should do today? We do not hear Him say; today I am too tired to proceed with the plan I told you about yesterday. Jesus had a three-year plan of what He came to earth to do and He disciplined himself to accomplish it.

Discipline applies to organizations as well. In a book by Jim Collins called *How The Mighty Fall*, the author describes how companies that were at one time the "most admired" began to falter and, in some cases, went out of business. Based on research by his team, Collins described the companies that persevered (did not falter) as having certain characteristics. First, they had "disciplined people" in their leadership. Second, they had "disciplined thought;" they did not try to go in many directions all at the same time. Third, there was "disciplined action" which followed the "disciplined thought." Action was consistent with thinking. Fourth, their goal was "building greatness to last" by building on what made the organization great at its beginning. They looked to their values and took a long-term view of how to discipline themselves.

How could this apply to us? We must know and think about our values which include our Christian faith. What are the talents and gifts God gave us? How might we utilize them? Will we discipline ourselves to follow those values (faith) and talents? Will we look for what has been good in our lives up to now and discipline ourselves to build on it? Greatness for us is to attain God's plan for us. Awareness of our values (faith), our talents and God's plan for us is the start. Accomplishment is a reflection of whether we are among the "disciplined people" to carry it out. Do you have the discipline to be the person God intended you to be?

STUDY QUESTIONS

1. Do you have a clear understanding of your values including your Christian faith? Write it out in a single page.
2. Do you know God's will for your life? If so, write it out in a single page. If not, how will you go about determining what God's will is?
3. Are you among the "disciplined people?" How might you go about increasing your discipline to help you achieve God's will for you?

From Jim Collins, *How The Mighty Fall* (HarperCollins, 2009)

369

"There is new life in the soil for every man. There is healing in the trees for tired minds, and for our overburdened spirits, there is strength in the hills, if only we lift up our eyes. Remember that nature is our great restorer." President Calvin Coolidge

KNOWING WHAT IS RIGHT

Our focus is <u>KNOWING</u> WHAT IS RIGHT. In another program there will be an emphasis on having the courage to <u>stand up</u> to others when their speech or action opposes what is right. We can be quick to criticize others when we disapprove of what they are doing or have done but it requires courage to stand up to them stating what you believe to be right.

But before we can take a stand for what is right, we have to figure out what <u>is</u> right. What we believe to be right is in our value system. This value system began in our infancy. We continually add to that value system as we grow older and mature. We gradually figure out what those around us, as well as society, consider to be right (the two could be very different) and we also determine as we mature whether to accept those guides to right behavior. Some children do not grow up in a family that demonstrates a desire to do what society says is right and what God has said is definitely right. But we have an inborn sense of right and wrong (when someone is kind to us we sense that is right but if someone harms us we sense it is wrong). The result is that each of has a unique value system.

So there are two issues here. <u>Knowing</u> what is right (from our value system) **and <u>deciding to follow</u> what is right.**

To know what is right we must first come to <u>understand and accept</u> what <u>is</u> right. This requires us to develop or accept some standard against which to measure various behaviors to determine what is right. The Bible is our best guide in finding standards against which behavior can be judged. The Bible contains some very specific directives about behavior such as The Ten Commandments but in other areas there are only general guidelines to tell us what is right. But the Bible does tell us "in all things love." When a behavior is done in genuine love (and meets the test of common sense), it is likely to be right behavior, assuming others do not misguide the person about how to demonstrate love. Any behavior motivated by hatred is bound to be wrong behavior.

For the second issue, deciding to follow what is right is a matter of commitment and courage. As Christians we must have a commitment to do what our faith tells is the right thing to do and to think. With a commitment to do what is right, we then need courage to act on our commitment. Skill, experience and opportunity are other factors with a role here. However, Christians tend to lack the courage to act on their faith commitments. We rationalize that we lack the skill or experience to talk to another person about their faith. We rationalize that no person has ever asked for help with his or her faith. Courage means taking the initiative using the gifts that we have without being overcome with how will this affect me. Courage means doing the right thing because it _is_ the right thing. Consider your gifts and use them to know what is right.

Knowing what is right should not be much of an issue with an active Christian. We have taken a stand on many issues in the past and stand firm on those issues. For others, the Bible gives sufficient direction in either the behaviors we are told to avoid and then the general direction to do unto others as we would have them do to us along with the commandment to love one another. When our Christian faith leads us to love one another, we are already close to knowing what is right and being the person God wants us to be. When the next opportunity arises, will you have the courage to speak up for what is right?

STUDY QUESTIONS

1. To what extent do you feel you have a good grasp on what is right?
2. To what extent do you feel you have a good grasp on what is wrong?
3. Recount a situation in which you took a stand for what you concluded was right even though it was not a popular decision.

363

CLEAN HEARTS AND CLEAR MINDS

A clean heart leads to a clear mind. Dr. Charles Stanley, pastor of First Baptist Church in Atlanta, made the comment, "We must have a clean heart to have a clear mind." We need to heed the exhortation given by the Apostle Peter in II Peter 1:13: "Therefore, with minds that are alert and fully sober, set your hope on the grace to be brought to you when Jesus Christ is revealed at His coming."

What does it mean to have a clean heart? It means that your conscience and sub-conscience are free of any secrets of sin from the present or past that you are not willing to share with others and for which you have not sought forgiveness. Even after God's forgiveness, it might mean the burden of past sin that you know was wrong and you are bothered by the fact that you entered into that sin. Once the sin is no longer present (even in our thoughts) and we have sought God's forgiveness, we need to move ahead in our lives to seek God's direction for the next part of our lives.

Maybe your heart isn't clean because there is sin there which is continuing and for which you have not sought God's forgiveness. If in doubt about whether a thought or action is sinful, consult the Bible. At least some part of the sin is going to be addressed by the Bible. Seek that clean heart in order to have a clear mind.

What is a clear mind? We have a clear mind when we can approach an issue and think about it objectively without harboring in the back of our mind that we have a preoccupation with a sin in our past or present or both. A clear conscience is a wonderful attribute. It allows the mind to do so much more than the mind that is cluttered with worries about regret or being found out or other negative outcomes.

Life is complex. We need the full capacities of our mind to cope with the challenges and opportunities before us. If your heart is not clean, today is the day to do something about it. First, seek God's forgiveness. Second, set the situation right. A clear mind will be your reward.

STUDY QUESTIONS

1.   Do you have a clean heart? Are there some small issues that keep your heart from being completely clean?

2.   A heart that is not clean could just involve what we are thinking about or what we see in videos or on TV such as porn. It could mean a selfish set of actions on our part. It could be something we continue to say about others. Does any of this apply to you?

3.   Think about the attributes of a clear mind. What can it help you to do?

160

"You were taught" . . . "to be made new in the attitude of your minds; and to put on the new self, created to be like God in true righteousness and holiness." Ephesians 4:20-24

"Be clear-minded and self-controlled so that you can pray. Above all, love each other deeply, because love covers over a multitude of sins. Offer hospitality to one another without grumbling. Each one should use whatever gift he has received to serve others faithfully administering God's grace in its various forms." 1 Peter 4:7-10

INVESTING IN YOURSELF

When we think of investing we tend to think of investing money in something so that there will be good financial return to us. Or we might think of an investment of time and energy in a project in hopes that the project will meet our expectations and return some benefit to us. What about investing in yourself to increase your capability to do the right things at the right time with the right results? How can you invest in yourself? Here are some thoughts.

1. **Learn** about something that you either don't understand or something in which you have limited knowledge. It could be done through a course, reading a book, planning an experience, talking to a person, watching something happen or discussing something with a group. It might mean research to write something for others to read. It might mean travel. It might mean creating or restoring something. We tend to learn when we get out of our box and do something constructively different. When you do something different, give thought <u>first</u> as to what you should do that would help you to learn. Then plan to share your new knowledge or experience with others.

2. **Volunteer** at your church, civic club, local school or some chartable organization. The new experience could give you a new perspective on many things in life including your perspective of who you are. Remember the television program in which the head of an organization goes to work in his or her organization at the lowest level in disguise? How did that leader's perspective change?

3. **Donate** some assets like money or possessions to a person or an organization that needs help. Get up close to those receiving it by going there instead of mailing a check to help you understand what they do. Your outlook on life will change.

4. **Talk with,** not to, people you don't normally exchange many words within the normal course of events. Stop and ask someone how <u>he or she</u> is doing and <u>listen</u> to what they say. Think about ways in which you might invest in <u>their</u> lives through showing an interest in them or helping them to achieve a goal that is important

to them. Include talking to a child or a teenager and listen intently to what they say.

5. **Read** the Bible on a regular basis. Consider such passages as I Timothy 6:18-19: "Command them to do good, to be rich in good deeds, and to be generous and willing to share. In this way they will lay up treasure for themselves as a firm foundation for the coming age, so that they may take hold of the life that is truly life."

Note that while you are investing in yourself, you are also investing in others. When investing in yourself, it also helps us to come closer to being the person God intended us to be. Yet notice in the suggestions above how much of the activity is reaching out to new information, new experiences, and new people. By reaching out we find new ways to extend our positive influence in the world. And when we positively impact other people, we magnify our efforts through the positive things that they in turn do for and with others.

An important part of you includes the gifts from God that each person receives. This unique set of gifts makes *you* unique. Discover how you are unique and then build upon it through education, experiences, contemplative thought and action. The more deeply you understand your potential and your interests, the greater the probability of discovering a new avenue of life. An investment of time and energy could create a new you. Take the time and energy to invest in yourself to move toward the person God wants you to be and the person who finds joy every day.

STUDY QUESTIONS

1. Sit down at your computer or with a piece of paper and think about some ways in which you might invest in yourself. Then set it aside and come back to it tomorrow to add the things that came to mind in the interim.

2. Take one item on the list above and give it careful consideration. Plan out how you will accomplish it.

CHAPTER TWO

WISDOM AND GOALS, MOTIVATION

Applying Wisdom, Setting Goals, Priorities, Motivation, Finishing Well, Passion, Decision Making, Attitude, Commitment, Hope, What We Need To Do, What You Do Next, What You Care Deeply About, Clarence Oddbody

SEEKING WISDOM

Seeking wisdom is an action we take, not something that just happens to us. If we are to have wisdom, we must seek it. Wisdom is the application of rational thought based on insight, perspective, knowledge and experience while lacking unfair bias. Rational thought means 1) starting with a realistic and careful assessment of the situation - knowing the facts that apply and 2} being able to remove from consideration that which is not pertinent to the situation. We tend to fail either partially or fully in completing these initial tasks. If the situation is not understood accurately, no resolution will be filled with wisdom. A wrong assessment (strongly influenced by emotion or bias, for example) will produce a wrong solution. It is here that we need to pray for wisdom. James 1:5 tells us: "If any of you lacks wisdom, you should ask God, who gives generously to all without finding fault, and it will be given to you." We need to acquire sufficient wisdom to assess a given situation.

Regarding #2 above, finding wisdom is often clouded by the opinions of others, distracting events, the setting, past events, words said, anxiety, emotion, prejudice and the forces of evil. It is possible only with God to remove all of these factors in seeking wisdom, but they must be recognized so as to counter their influence when thinking to seek wisdom.

Rational thought applies wisdom to possible solutions. We can flee, fight, use emotion (or prejudice) or we can think. Wisdom is likely to be absent in the first three even though circumstances might require them. For example, if the building is on fire, flee is probably the best option. When we think about what the nature of the situation is and then what we want to come from that situation, that is seeking wisdom. As Christians, our natural disposition is to love one another (1 John 3:11) and if we are able to avoid emergency situations, we are in a position to calmly think about how Jesus might have faced the situation. That is seeking wisdom.

Wisdom requires thinking, the processing of many variables in the mind. In applying wisdom, our actions will normally follow our value system (at times our actions are outside of our value system). Seeking wisdom requires accepting truth even when it is counter to our bias. Following our value system, our actions are less likely to be regretted later because wisdom helps us to understand what is right and what is wrong. The application of wisdom, however, also requires motivation, courage and self-confidence.

Wisdom requires knowing and keeping in mind the intended outcome while keeping emotions and bias under control. For example, if a child accidentally spills a glass of milk, we can respond with anger because of the work it might create for us, or we can respond in love, understanding that coordination and other skills are what we are attempting to help the child to learn.

Emotion, experience, learning, perspective and values all enter into how we will act in a given situation. However, if we follow the advice of James 1:5 (quoted earlier) in seeking wisdom, we and those around us will be happier with our actions and their impact. Are you seeking wisdom?

STUDY QUESTIONS

1. When you seek wisdom, where do you begin? Some of the Scriptures you might consult are: Pr 9:9, 16:23, 13:20, 13:1, 9:8, 3:7, 29:3, 23:23, 13:10, 11:2, 4:7, 3:13, 1Kings 3:12, 4:23, James 3:13, Isa 11:2, and Ps 111:10.
2. Think about how you balance wisdom and emotion in your life.
3. What are the factors that will at times keep you from acting based on wisdom in your life? Are there means by which you might limit these factors?

388

SETTING PRIORITIZED GOALS

We tend to accomplish more when we have goals. Goals, clearly thought through and stated, help us to start the process by getting us to think about what it will take to accomplish the goal. What resources including money will we need to get it done, how much time will it take, what other parts of our life including our family and friends will be affected by this goal and how much do I really want to get this done are the questions we have to answer to ourselves. This last one, our motivation, is a strong factor in whether this goal will ever be accomplished. We need to distinguish between the things that we really want to see done and those things that would be nice if they were accomplished. The second group is desired but without the same level of motivation. There are times when motivation runs low but we know we must persevere. This is when discipline supplements motivation to get it done.

The Book of Proverbs in 21:5 has some encouragement for us. We could make this a motto on the wall: "The plans of the diligent lead to profit as surely as haste leads to poverty." There is ample evidence that success comes out of good planning. We should pray about each of the goals we set.

Goals should have several characteristics. 1) We must believe that we could possibly accomplish the goal within our time, talent and resources even if it is a reach. 2) The goal should be written down forcing us to think through all aspects of that goal and to give us the opportunity to read it again and again reminding us of the goal. 3) We must prioritize among our various goals. Goals are accomplished only after the basic needs of life are met and we tend to have many goals at the same time. Some of these goals can be accomplished quickly and others might take years like earning a college degree. Really big goals need to be broken down into parts to state where we will start – what are the first steps? Some goals are going to be more important than others.

This is where setting priorities comes in. The best way to accomplish goals is to determine what do I need to do today. Which parts of larger goals can go on your to do list for today? Even when there is a daily list, there are some items on the list that are more critical than others. Step 2 for tomorrow cannot be done then unless step one gets done today. Write down your big goals and then determine what steps should I take today to move toward the realization of those goals. Set priorities among your goals and discipline yourself to follow those prioritized goals. It will make you a happier camper.

STUDY QUESTIONS

1. What are the big goals you have for the rest of your life?
2. Which of those goals are the most important to you?
3. Prioritize your goals while considering your time, your talents and your resources.

48

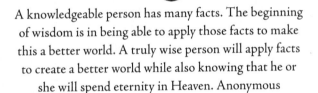

A knowledgeable person has many facts. The beginning of wisdom is in being able to apply those facts to make this a better world. A truly wise person will apply facts to create a better world while also knowing that he or she will spend eternity in Heaven. Anonymous

"Commit to the Lord whatever you do, and your plans will succeed." Proverbs 16:3

"If we are to guard against ignorance and remain free, it is the responsibility of every American to be informed." President Thomas Jefferson

VISUALIZING YOUR GOALS

Have you ever heard it said, "If you can't visualize a goal (something you want to have happen), you can't make it happen regardless of your effort?" Achieving a goal is closely related to knowing precisely what the goal is more than the amount of energy you put into achieving the goal. In Luke 14:28, we read: "Suppose one of you wants to build a tower. Won't you first sit down and estimate the cost to see if you have enough money to complete it?"

Why is visualizing your goal or goals so important? When we visualize, we picture in our minds what something might look like. We see the details. The greater the detail of visualization of a goal, the greater the likelihood that the goal will come to pass. If we write down what we are visualizing, we increase our chances of accomplishing the goal even more. Writing it down will help us to visualize as we search for the appropriate words to describe what the mind is seeing. When we visualize more precisely, we can then see more clearly what it is that we need to do <u>today</u> to make the goal come about in the future.

So what would you like see happen? What are your dreams? Can you visualize what it is that you would like to have happen? To what level of detail? Are you willing to do <u>today</u> what that goal requires? Start by visualizing in the greatest level of detail possible what your dream is that would make you a more active contributor to making this a better world.

STUDY QUESTIONS

1. Write down three to five of your personal goals?
2. Take one of these goals, and visualize what it would look like when completed. Sketch it out if that will help.
3. Do you like the picture you are seeing? What does it do for your motivation? 147

"Wisdom must be sought in order to be found. It doesn't arrive wrapped in a bow on the doorstep of your Christian life." Pastor Dr. David Jeremiah

"Do not store up for yourselves treasures on earth, where moth and rust destroy, and where thieves break in and steal. But store up for yourselves treasures in Heaven, where moth and rust do not destroy, and where thieves do not break in and steal. For where your treasure is, there your heart will be also." Matthew 6:19-21

"No man is happy who does not think himself so." Publilius Syrus (85-42 B C)

"Being true to Him is staying teachable regardless of much you know." Pastor Dr. Laura Brantley

WHAT'S ON YOUR BUCKET LIST?

The movie Bucket List has prompted many people to think about what might be on THEIR bucket list. This is being written while I am completing an item on my bucket list – a train trip across Canada from Winnipeg to Prince Rupert on the Pacific Ocean.

What is a bucket list? It is composed of things that interest us and that we would like to do during our lifetime. As life progresses we both see things that might go on the list and at the same time perceive that the time remaining in life with good health is diminishing. As a result, we make up a list and give thought as to how we might complete the items we have listed.

Why would something be on our bucket list? First, it is something we have never done before but, second, have thought about more than once as something that would we would enjoy doing. Third, it tends to be something that will take a special effort to complete and, fourth, has a touch of the unusual. Most other people won't have the same items on their list.

Is becoming a Christian and joining a church on your bucket list? If you have already made that move, maybe the bucket list could include a greater involvement in your Church such as Sunday School teaching or serving on a board or committee. Financial support of your Church could grow as your personal finances have been blessed. Is that on the bucket list?

Consider how you might expand your bucket list to serving others. Remember how Jesus (Matthew 25:31-40) separated the sheep and goats. He then said, "Come, you who are blessed by my Father, take your inheritance, the Kingdom prepared for you." Jesus explained that when they served others they had served Him. But then they professed that they did not know when they had served Him, Jesus explained, "'…whatever you did for one of the least of these, you did for Me'" (Matthew 25:40).

Are there some things that could go on your bucket list including the "least of these"? Is there something you have thought about that you would like to do some day? Has God prompted you in your prayers to take some specific action? Take a piece of paper or your computer and start a list. Work on it over several days because not every item will come to mind right away. Now once the list is complete, think about <u>which one will I do first?</u>

STUDY QUESTIONS

1. Do you already have a bucket list? How much of it is completed? Are there activities in progress?
2. After reading the above, is there something you want to add to the bucket list?
3. Once you have a bucket list, consider how well it is serving God. 55

"If we let our problems define our situation we are unlikely to see the opportunities that come when we focus on purpose. Clarifying our purpose can let us out of our problems and give us meaning." Robert Quinn

"Take care of what is difficult while it is still easy, and deal with what will become big while it is yet small." Lao-Tzu (604-531 B C)

"Character is like a tree and reputation is like a shadow. The shadow is what we think of it; the tree is the real thing." President Abraham Lincoln

"A good name is more desirable than great riches, to be esteemed is better than silver or gold." Proverbs 22:1

IF YOU KNOW WHAT YOU WANT

What happens when you know what you want? Take two scenarios. In one scenario a person is interviewing for a job and is asked where would you like to be in five years? The person answered by saying I would like to have your job. In the second scenario, a person is asked the same question and answered by saying I don't know. In the second case the person was told to come back when they figured out the answer.

Do you know what you want in your personal life, in your career or in your relationship with God? Most people are frustrated with life because happiness has not been delivered to them in a neat package on the timetable that was convenient for them. If this fits you, maybe the real source of your frustration with life is that you haven't yet figured out what you want from life. You haven't determined what is really important to you. What is really important to you is based on your values.

So what are your values? What do you believe in? What would make you really happy? Don't say a lot of money because money is only the medium to acquire something else. What is the "something else"?

You have probably heard the adage that says, "If you don't know where you are going, any road will take you there."

Turn to prayer. God has a plan for you and you need to know about it. Look at Proverbs 19:21: "Many are the plans in a person's heart, but it is the Lord's purpose that prevails." We must surrender ourselves to God to follow what God knows is best for us. One prayer probably won't do it. Pray continuously for the direction needed in life. If we don't pray to seek God's guidance, we could find ourselves drifting in an ocean of problems without a sail. Every plan should begin and end with God in mind.

If you know what you want like the person in the first interview described above, you will learn which road to take, when to take it, how to prepare for your journey and how to relate to people on the way. If you know what you want, you are more likely to obtain your goal. Compare this to the person who complains about life, blames others for his or her situation and doesn't know what to do to make life better. Which of these two people do **you** want to be?

STUDY QUESTIONS

1. What was the main difference between the two people in the interviews?
2. What do you believe in? What are your values?
3. If you achieve what you want, will you be happy? 111

"What lies behind us and what lies before us are tiny matters compared to what lies within us." Ralph Waldo Emerson

"Don't be afraid of what you want. This is your time. The barriers are down." Morgan Freeman

"Our three healthy keys to the good life are someone to love, something to do and something to look forward to." Mayo Clinic

"Life is no brief candle for me. It a sort of splendid torch which I've got ahold of for the moment, and I want to make it burn as brightly as possible before handing it off to future generations." Bob Buford in *Half Time, Moving from Success to Significance*

RUNNING OUT OF DREAMS

The other day a song was played on the radio in which the words were "I'm runnin' out of dreams." What a sad statement to be made by anyone. When we run out of dreams for the future, we see a very bleak or at least a very routine future. This program is sent to prisoners each week who are encouraged to have dreams – to think of the future – even when they know that others very tightly control their immediate future. But society can only put your physical body in prison and not your mind. If your mind is in prison, you put it there and you can get it out.

As we pursue our dreams we need to always remember the words of the Lord through Jeremiah in Chapter twenty-nine, verse eleven: "For I know the plans I have for you, declares the Lord, "plans to prosper you and not to harm you, plans to give you hope and a future..." Pray, trust in His admonitions and allow God to help build your dreams.

Hope needs to be present in everyone. We can have hope for our own immediate and long-term future AND we can have hope for the short-term and long-term future of others. Corporate executive Armand Hammer at the age of 95 decided he would plant trees. He obviously had a hope that they would grow and that others would benefit from them. His hope would be limited for himself due to his age but he also had a hope for a better world for others that he might contribute to while on earth. Think of hope for both yourself and for others.

Hope is the essence of which dreams are made. We are by our nature optimistic beings. We think of what tomorrow could be for ourselves and for others. When we think of others, we can include our immediate family but it can also include the hope for larger issues such as world peace.

The next opportunity you have when not driving a car or busy fixing a meal, you might sit down with a piece of paper or a blank page on your computer and write down what comes to mind about YOUR dreams. Think first about yourself because dreams for others can often get started from our personal dreams. You don't have to share these with others – at least not yet. But you will want to share them later after you have thought through what should be on your page.

Then think about your dreams for others. Some of your personal dreams can be the basis for what you can do for others. Think near you and think far away for more global issues. The process of writing your dreams can be exciting for you. Unlike the song, you will find that you have many dreams. Now, where is that piece of paper?

STUDY QUESTIONS

1. Do you have dreams (aspirations) for the future? How many of them are you able to describe on a screen or on paper?
2. What is the biggest, most important, dream you have for the future? What are you doing about it today?
3. In what ways is God involved in your plans (dreams) for the future? 98A

"A goal not set will be a goal not achieved." Anonymous

"The world is but a canvas to our imaginations." Henry David Thoreau

"There is nothing in a caterpillar that tells you it's going to be a butterfly." Buckminster Fuller

"Empty pockets never held anyone back. Only empty heads and empty hearts can do that." Norman Vincent Peale

HOPE

Evangelist Billy Graham made the statement, "Perhaps the greatest psychological and spiritual need that all people have is the need for hope." This appears in his book *Hope for the Troubled Heart*. Dr. Graham goes on to say, "Hope is both biologically and psychologically vital to man. Men and women must have hope, and yet a great part of our world today is living without it." He continues by quoting a professor of psychiatry, "Hope, like faith and a purpose in life, is medicinal. This is not a statement of belief, but a conclusion proved by (a) meticulously controlled scientific experiment."

So what do we learn from these statements? Hope is essential for both the Christian and the non-believer. Our only hope might be that our present world will continue. Or our hope might be for something that is bigger, better or more pleasant than what we have today. Either way, we have hope that the future will have at least some rays of sunshine for us and for those we love. Our hope could extend to the world around us or even all of God's creatures. When we hope, it is sometimes irrational but we cling to that hope. When the future looks bleak or when it seems nothing could go wrong, either way that view of the future is based on hope.

As Christians we are given hope regardless of our circumstances on earth. Edward Mote wrote these words in the well-known hymn:

My hope is built on nothing less than Jesus blood and righteousness,
I dare not trust the sweetest frame but wholly lean on Jesus name.
On Christ the solid rock I stand.
All other ground is sinking sand.

Jesus will bless all who come to Him and He will never turn away. John 14:27 adds "Do not let your hearts be troubled and do not be afraid." Jesus comforts us by saying, "Lo, I am with you always."

Billy Graham in the book mentioned earlier says our hope is in Heaven. John 14:2-3 tells us the words of Jesus: "I am going there to prepare a place for you. And if I go . . .I will come back and take you to be with me that you also may be where I am."

In order to have this hope, there is one thing we must do. In John 14:6 Jesus is quoted as saying, "I am the way and the truth and the life. No one comes to the Father except through me."

Edward Mote the songwriter quoted earlier, wrote:

> When He shall come with trumpet sound,
> O may I then in Him be found.

How about you? Where will you be found? No one has the hope of Jesus as a companion now and of Heaven later except through Jesus Christ.

STUDY QUESTIONS

1. Describe the hope that exists in your life.
2. Is hope for the future an important part of your life?
3. Are you taking steps today that will ensure that your hopes for the future can be realized?

193

"The world is but a canvas to our imaginations." Henry David Thoreau

"There is nothing in a caterpillar that tells you it's going to be a butterfly." Buckminster Fuller

"Empty pockets never held anyone back. Only empty heads and empty hearts can do that." Norman Vincent Peale

HOPE IS NOT A STRATEGY

All of us hope for many things. Many of the things we hope for do not materialize. We are typically disappointed when our hopes do not come true. We tend to blame bad luck or other people for our disappointment. A hope tends to be vague as in a passing thought. Hopes are seldom written down or described to other people. We seldom think them through to clarify the ramifications that would be present if our hope came true. We tend not to want to put much energy into our hopes, often accepting defeat even before we have clearly defined our hope.

In order to have more of our hopes come true, there are some things that we personally can do. Let's consider some of them.

1. GIVE DEFINITION TO OUR HOPE Exactly what is it that we hope will happen or come true. A good first step is to write it down. Put down every thought that comes to mind about this hope. Complete sentences are not necessary. After you have done this, look through your notes to determine what the essential characteristics are of this hope. What other things are secondary. Then rewrite it into a synopsis of what your notes say. Pray that God will help you define your hope and pray that the hope is within God's will.

2. CONSIDER STRATEGIES FOR ACCOMPLISHING THE HOPE Strategies are methods, the how to accomplish something. Strategies normally have a specific order in which they must occur. If the hope is to be a concert pianist, strategy one might be to start piano lessons or acquire access to a piano.

3. PLACE STRATEGIES IN A TIME FRAME Not all strategies to obtain a goal can be done on day one. There might be a number of piano lessons before the strategy of having a piano recital is possible. To make these strategies more likely to be achieved, put them in a time order. What must be done right now, what is next month, next year, in two years, later time frames? But remember that no strategy has value without the hope being present.

4. DISCIPLINE OURSELVES TO FOLLOW THE STRATEGIES Strategies are of no value if we lack the discipline to follow every strategy on schedule. Hopes fade when discipline is lacking.
5. TELL OTHERS ABOUT THE HOPE Tell other people who believe in you about what you hope for. Give them the opportunity to both open doors for you and to encourage you.
6. DIRECTLY FACE YOUR BARRIERS One or more barriers have dashed many hopes. It could be a person, it could be where you are; it could be your background in which you are not connected to anyone who can help you; it could be a lack of self confidence; it could be time; it could be health issues. Whatever the barrier, consider how you can minimize the barriers.
7. PLACE THE HOPE ON THE WALL Place it in writing where you will see it constantly to remind you, such as on the refrigerator door. You might even post the next strategies for accomplishing the hope on a page where many will see it.

Be determined. Pray about it. If what you hope for is good for you, good for others and pleasing to God, these strategies can help you achieve that hope.

STUDY QUESTIONS

1. If there is something you are hoping for, define it by writing it down on a piece of paper or on a computer screen. Then record your other thoughts about the concept. Finally, read though all of this to get a good handle on exactly what your hope is about.
2. Maybe someone close to you has a strong hope. What can you do to open doors for them or encourage them?
3. Think about something you hoped for in the past. Did it come true? If so, what were the factors that made it happen? If it didn't, what factors caused it not to happen?

Read more: https://www.whatchristianswanttoknow.com/bible-verses-about-hope-20-uplifting-scripture-quotes/#ixzz5ysJsQjbR

156

CLARENCE ODDBODY, AS2

We are bringing back an interesting character from our memory. In the film, *It's A Wonderful Life,* **Clarence Oddbody, AS2,** helps George Bailey to see what the world would have been like if he had never lived. It takes George quite some time to understand that many good things in Bedford Falls came about only because of what he had already done in his life. Clarence was motivated by wanting to help someone so that he could get his "wings." Yet George Bailey was not an easy person to help with his unwillingness to accept the reality that Clarence showed to him.

There are some interesting attributes in these two characters. Clarence Oddbody had only one purpose, that of being able to help someone to qualify him for getting his wings. As you look at all the things that he did, everything had this single focus. He succeeded in accomplishing his goal. How many of us have such a clear focus on what we want to accomplish? There is a direct relationship between the clarity of focus in our lives and our chances of accomplishing what we have set out to do. A focus is likely to have several parts with each of them important and coming together for the overall accomplishment. In the case of Clarence, the focus was helping George but saving him from drowning was only part of it. Showing him the town without his efforts was another part. Both contributed to the focus.

In the case of George Bailey, early in the film he stated that his goal was to go to college, make a lot of money and to get away from Bedford Falls. Why did he fail in all three of these? His focus was at odds with his real value system which emphasized his father, the Building and Loan Association and the people of Bedford Falls. When these three values pulled on him, he gave in. He honored his father, he saved the Building and Loan and he expressed his love for the people of the town.

In the case of Clarence Oddbody, AS2, his focus and his values were consistent with one another. There was only one thing important to him and he concentrated on it until he succeeded. George Bailey had an original focus inconsistent with his values. He succeeded but only after his focus was changed to be consistent with his values. Keeping your focus is addressed in

Proverbs 4:23 which reads, "Above all else, guard your heart, for everything you do flows from it."

Think about your goals, your focus. How consistent is it with your values, what is really important to you? Develop goals consistent with your values and your success rate will improve. In case you are still wondering, Clarence Oddbody explained that AS2 stood for Angel Second Class (doesn't have his wings yet). Do you have your wings yet?

STUDY QUESTIONS 319

1. In what ways do you resemble Clarence Oddbody, AS2?
2. In what ways do you resemble George Bailey?
3. Think about what lessons can be learned from "It's A Wonderful Life."

"From the mouth of the righteous comes the fruit of wisdom, but a perverse tongue will be silenced." Proverbs 10:31

"The wise in heart accept commands, but a chattering fool comes to ruin." Proverbs 10:8

"The jaws of power are always open to devour, and her arm is always stretched out, if possible, to destroy the freedom of thinking, speaking, and writing." President John Adams

THINGS WE NEED TO DO

After 13 or 14 years of assisting a Kindergarten teacher (the wonderful Mrs. Gilliland) every Tuesday, I observed many of the basics of life that we should learn early and keep as we age. Your own Kindergarten experience might have been a lot like mine of playing with blocks of wood and taking naps on a rug. But Kindergarten today is an amazing place where at 5 (6 by the end of the year), children learn not only how to write a sentence and deal with numbers up to 100, they learn how to relate to other people. Many of the children have had little opportunity to interact with children their own age when they enter Kindergarten or have not been in a group situation where they are to follow directions.

Robert Fulghum wrote a book on what we need to know we learned in Kindergarten. Some of things he mentions are: "share with others, play fair, don't hit people, put things back where you found them, clean up your own mess, don't take things that aren't yours, say you're sorry when you hurt somebody, wash your hands before you eat, flush, live a balanced life – learn some and think some and draw and paint and sing and dance and play and work every day some, take a nap every afternoon, when you go out in the world, watch out for traffic, hold hands and stick together, be aware of wonder, remember the little seed in the Styrofoam cup, and then remember the Dick and Jane books and the first word you learned – the biggest word of all, LOOK."

Reflecting on the many years I had in Kindergarten with Mrs. G (as the students called her), I have added some other things we learned in Kindergarten along with some that we need to learn early in life and then keep them as guides for later. They are: Always tell the truth but you don't have to tell everyone about all of your warts, be nice to others, smile when you see others including strangers but never go with a person you do not know unless it is a policeman, continue to make new friends, think about who needs your help and then provide it, others watch us – make sure you are a good example, create something that comes from your imagination, smell and enjoy the beauty of flowers, hand the scissors to others with the handle first, clean your plate, eat what is good for you but have a little chocolate from time to time, return what you borrowed, listen carefully – seek to understand before you act, stand up for what is right even if uncomfortable, if you must stand on a chair place the back of the chair to the wall, get enough sleep, get some exercise, wear a helmet when you ride a bike, say thank you when someone does something for you, follow principles and laws instead of just preferences, never use profanity or vulgarity, honor your Mother and Father, listen to and respect your teachers and other adults, learn something significant every day, seek ways to have everyone who meets you today to be happy with the experience, enjoy multiple kinds of music, read books including the Bible, read biographies of people you admire, appreciate and learn about history, develop your God given talents and gifts, work hard and finish what you start, don't confuse the means with the ends (the end is your goal but the means must be ethical and kind), enjoy God's masterpieces in nature, take care of your health, don't let your attitude contradict your principles and faith, set both short-term and long-term goals, get the best education, learn from your experiences, dress according to where you are and the nature of the event, think about the future and not just today, and pray often to seek God's counsel and forgiveness for your shortcomings. Please God, help others, live to your potential and smile some.

The Apostle Paul said in II Corinthians 9:6: "Remember this: Whoever sows sparingly will also reap sparingly, and whoever sows generously will also reap generously." These are some guidelines for a bountiful life.

STUDY QUESTIONS

1. Identify three of the guidelines above that particularly strike you as significant. Explain why they are significant.
2. What guidelines would you add?
3. What did you learn from your Kindergarten experience?

380

GOALS, MOTIVATION, DISCIPLINE

Our topic is goal setting, having motivation and having discipline, in that order. A goal could be 1) something I must do, 2) something I need to do (maybe because a parent, spouse or boss has requested it), 3) something I would like to get done, or 4) something I would like to do some day. The fourth category has little chance of ever happening. It would have to move up at least one category in order to happen. Category 3 could happen with some discipline. An item in category 2 will happen if the "need" is strong. If the parent, spouse or boss says, "Did you get that done?" it might push the item up to category 1. But even a category 1 goal, "something I must do," will not happen unless there is motivation and discipline.

In order for any goal to be accomplished it must be clear and distinct. To live a better life or to lose weight are not clear goals. A goal must be clear enough that there will be no doubt about when it has been accomplished. A goal of losing 30 pounds from my present weight by July 1 is clearer. A serious goal must be written down. Written goals tend to be more precise (use numbers and dates) and do not change as our memory of the goals fade or are rationalized. Put the written copy where you will see it often.

Motivation is the intensity of our intention to get the goal accomplished. It might be a step toward a greater goal such as finishing college so that a desired career could be started. Motivation could come from within us because of our values – how important it is to us personally. Motivation could also come from external sources – I better get this done before it rains or I really want to please my spouse before he or she returns. Motivation could also be what drives us to avoid doing something like smoking.

Discipline might be the most difficult part. Many New Year's resolutions are lost due to the lack of discipline. This means we will do things (or deprive ourselves of them) regardless of our discomfort to accomplish the goal. Discipline is aided by having another person to whom we are accountable for the success of our goal or who is working on a similar goal with us. Rationalization becomes more difficult when the friend helps or encourages us. Discipline tells us that even when we lack adequate personal motivation, we must just make ourselves do it.

When you select goals, consider them carefully. Avoid writing an "if" beside each goal because that could be your escape clause. Decide that you <u>will</u> complete your goals. Go through several drafts. Then sleep on it. But then take the final written version that is sufficiently specific with dates for accomplishment and what resources you will need, build up sufficient motivation (motivation will grow as you visualize the goals while you prepare them) and then discipline yourself to goal achievement (visualize the end result you desire). There will be many discouraging times and rationalizations to drop a goal along the way. But if you persevere, you will be pleased with the result.

In Luke 14:28 Jesus encouraged us to plan ahead: "For which of you, intending to build a tower, sitteth not down first, and counts the cost, whether he has sufficient to finish it? Consider also the words of Proverbs 6:6 which says, "Go to the ant, you sluggard; consider its ways and be wise!" God encourages us to set goals in order to create the world pleasing to Him.

STUDY QUESTIONS

1. There are probably a number of goals in your head that you would like to accomplish. Select one of them and write it down. Then read it again to make corrections including making it more succinct. Sleep on it and then read it again tomorrow to make further corrections.
2. How strong is your motivation to accomplish this goal? What lengths are you willing to go? If there are steps you must take to prepare for this goal, what are they and are you willing to tackle them?
3. How is your self-discipline? If you decide to do something, are you likely to let others talk you out of it, or are you apt to rationalize when the going gets tough? The people who accomplish a lot in life are not necessarily the smartest people; they are the people who possess the clearest goals, have very strong motivation and have greater discipline that most people.

256

PASSION, NOT PENSION

Consider having a passion rather than a pension. Dennis Kimbro once said:

> Remember, a job is something you do for money, but a career is something you do out of love. Chase your passion, not your pension.

The first thought in this quote is that we should seek a career, not just a job. A job will not lead to the satisfaction that a career will. A career suggests that we are doing something that utilizes our gifts and skills and that provides some continuity toward larger goals over many years.

That which becomes a passion for us could be our career. But we can have many passions, things that we really care about. Our most important passion should be our Christian faith and all of the implications it carries including love of one another. In addition to our Christian faith, love for one another, and our career, we could have a passion about our church, our family, our friends, special interests and multiple other aspects of life. When we have some passions about life, we are more likely to enjoy life. When we have passions and enjoy life, we are more likely to make life enjoyable for those around us. When we make others happy, they in turn are more likely to enhance the quality of the people they meet as well as our lives.

The other part of the quote mentions a pension. The writer is urging us not to go through life thinking about when we can collect a pension and no longer have to do more than the minimum to live. Living for the pension suggests doing the minimum through life. Doing the minimum is likely to be a boring and uneventful life.

What are your passions? Are you pursuing them? If not, what will it take to begin the pursuit? The passion for your Christian faith needs to be the starting point. Seek first His Kingdom. Then pursue the other passions in your life. Don't just wait for the pension.

STUDY QUESTIONS

1. Is your Christian faith one of your passions? Are you excited about your faith?
2. What are your other passions? Make a list.
3. Is there a passion you listed in #2 that you are not pursuing currently? If so, what are you going to do about it?

210

"Far better it is to dare mighty things, to win glorious triumphs, even though checkered by failure, than to take rank with those poor spirits who neither enjoy much nor suffer much, because they live in the gray twilight that knows not victory nor defeat." Theodore Roosevelt

"If you want to be happy, be happy." Leo Tolstoy

"No one can make you feel inferior without your consent." Eleanor Roosevelt

"Whoever heeds life-giving correction will be at home with the wise." Proverbs 15:31

ATTITUDE

Have you thought about the importance of attitude? Attitude is how we approach everything in life. We can be optimistic, inquisitive, skeptical, bored, negative and a number of other approaches to an idea, a situation or a person. That attitude determines much of the outcome of that interchange. If our attitude is such that we are sure we don't like a person before we meet them, it is limited as to what they can do which might change that attitude. We often prejudge a situation or person to our own detriment thus ending an opportunity for what might have been a positive experience.

A positive attitude can have the effect of taking 1 + 1 and making it equal three. The positive attitude can add to the situation thus creating more than was there initially.

A man and a woman who are married and have a positive outlook on life and each other are not likely to ever end in divorce. Through their positive outlook they will find a way to overcome those problems that all of us face at one time or another.

As you wake up tomorrow morning, you might resolve to have a positive attitude about the day in front of you. It will make your day more pleasant not only for you but for everyone around you. You are more likely to accomplish that which you set out to do and give you a sense of satisfaction in what you have done.

The Bible encourages us about having the right attitude. Proverbs 17:22 exhorts us: "A cheerful heart is good medicine, but a crushed spirit dries up the bones." There is no cost to this, just a choice by our free will as to the kind of person we choose to be. Decide today to be what you know you want to be!

STUDY QUESTIONS

1. Evaluate your attitude. How cheerful or grumpy are you?
2. How could 1 + 1 come to equal 3?
3. Attitude is one of the few things we can personally control. How are you doing in the control seat on attitude?

38

"Ambition is the subtlest beast of the intellectual and moral field. It is wonderfully adroit in concealing itself from its owner." President John Adams

"Where there is strife, there is pride, but wisdom is found in those who take advice." Proverbs 13:10

"The man who can look upon a crisis without being willing to offer himself upon the altar of his country is not fit for public trust." President Millard Fillmore

PRUDENT DECISION-MAKING

Let's think about the nature of prudent decision-making. We have opportunities to make decisions every moment of our waking lives. Most of them are momentary, small decisions but some of those small issues set the stage for a pattern of behavior that could have many consequences. Nonetheless, let's look at some of our major decisions.

One of our options when the opportunity for a decision is in front of us is no action at all. However, we must remember that no decision is still a decision. We have elected to take no action at that point and accepted the status quo. We might not have the opportunity to make that decision again. We have closed some doors.

Another option is to make a bad decision. A bad decision can come from acting too early or too late. It often comes from not taking the time to understand the decision in front of us causing us to choose from only from poor choices. Seek clarity when faced with making a decision by knowing the essence of the decision but also the nature of the alternatives from which you can choose. We can also make a stupid decision caused by not thinking through the implications of our action or making a decision based on personal whims or just bad assumptions. Bad decisions do not contribute to reaching long-term goals.

Prudent decision-making requires a careful understanding of the issue and a careful understanding of the options related to that issue. Prudent decision-making also requires courage. Prudent or wise decisions seldom are easy decisions to make in both the difficulty of finding the right answer as well as having the courage to make that decision in the best way. Prudent decision-making is always in keeping with God's will so we are helped in decision making by prayer. Prudent decision-making is most likely when we consult others, seek information and take time (such as overnight) to make a decision. However, an otherwise wise decision made too early or too late can be a very unwise choice. Clear thinking is essential for prudent decision-making – find a quiet place to think through a decision before taking action that will close off some options. Avoiding pressure from others as much as possible helps prudent decision-making.

You might think of other pieces of advice to lead to prudent decision-making. But lead into big decisions with the right attitude, self-confidence and ensuring that the decision will assist, rather than hinder, long-term goals. Let every decision help you move toward the future world that you are building today.

STUDY QUESTIONS

1. Are you bothered by a recent decision you made wondering if it will help you reach longer-term goals? Think it through and consider how you might make the effect of that decision more beneficial.
2. Of the suggestions for prudent decision-making above, which ones are you using currently?
3. What is the area in which you are most likely to stumble in making big decisions?

153

"If money is your hope for independence, you will never have it. The only real security that a man can have in this world is a reserve of knowledge, experience and ability." Henry Ford

Failing to make a decision is still a decision. That opportunity might not come by again.

WHEN YOU GET TO THE FORK IN THE ROAD

Yogi Berra, outstanding catcher for the New York Yankees and later a manager for the New York Mets and the Yankees, is often quoted as saying, "When you get to the fork in the road, take it." Yogi wrote a book called "Take It." In it he offers some sage advice to the reader. While many have laughed at this statement, "When you get to the fork in the road, take it," there really is some sound advice in it. In his book, Yogi goes on to say, "Make a firm decision. Make sure it feels right. Learn from the choice you make. Don't second-guess yourself – there's no need to give yourself ulcers. But my advice on big life decisions is to get advice if you can. Talk it over with a parent, a mentor, a teacher or a coach." All of this is from Yogi Berra. He is saying that when you get to the fork in the road, don't just stand there. Make a decision. <u>Remember that failure to make a decision is still a decision.</u>

Another piece of Yogi Berra advice is this: "Even when you get older, you should never be a know-it-all. You can always learn from someone else's experience." As we get older we can draw upon our education and experience to make wiser decisions. But sometimes we don't learn from our experiences **or** the experiences of others.

An interesting comment by Yogi Berra is "I learned a long time ago that losing is a learning experience. It teaches you humility. It teaches you to work harder. It's also a powerful motivator." He adds, "Accept the losses and learn from them." How many times have each of us lost at something and then proceeded to do the same thing while expecting to win next time. We need to consider what we learned from losing.

We all face competition. Yogi Berra commented, "Competition at all levels should be a good, healthy thing. I think you find out a lot about yourself as a competitor. Can you rise to meet a challenge? Do you take yourself too seriously? Can you congratulate whoever beat you?" We can let the loss of a deal or a sale cripple us. Yogi is suggesting that we learn from our challenges, whether we win or lose, and face another day as a better person.

Decision-making is often difficult for us. We might not see the alternatives very clearly. We might feel rushed to make a decision with which we are uncomfortable. There are times when we need to sleep on a decision. Doing so might help us see options we did not visualize the day before. It is important to make wise decisions. John 14:6 tells us about the big decision we all must make which is to accept Jesus Christ as Savior because He is... "the way and the truth and the life." Like other decisions put off, failure to make this decision will mean not spending eternity in Heaven. Are you putting off this and other decisions? Are you at the "fork in the road?" What challenge, win or lose, has taught you something in the last week?

STUDY QUESTIONS

1. Are there certain kinds of decisions you have difficulty making on a timely basis? Why is that? When is that a positive?
2. What are your favorite Yogi Berra quotes? Why is that?
3. Have you made the decision mentioned in John 14:6?

90A

"Wisdom is found on the lips of the discerning, but a rod is for the back of one who has no sense." Proverbs 10:13

COMMITMENT

What commitments have you made lately? Did you intend to have that commitment continue until the activity was completed or at least your role in it? Often we make commitments without much thought thinking that sounds OK so I can say I'll commit to it. Sometimes we don't use the word commit, but instead might say, "OK, I'll go along with that," or "that sounds good to me." If the other person assumes that is a commitment on your part to whatever it is that is being suggested or proposed, in their mind at least, you have made a commitment. If you do not follow through on that commitment, your relationship with that person or group will be damaged with you being seen as a person who does keep his or her commitments. The Bible speaks of commitment as "do not give up." The Apostle Paul exhorts us in Galatians 6:9: "Let us not become weary in doing good, for at the proper time we will reap a harvest if we do not give up."

Lesson #1 here is to make it clear if you are committing to something. Don't leave it ambiguous, with others possibly having a different understanding from yours. Lesson #2 is to be very clear about the boundaries to your commitment and the time frame in which they need to be accomplished. Repeat back to the person as to the extent and time frame of your commitment.

Lesson #3 is to think about what this commitment means to you. What will you need to do to follow through on a commitment and when does this need to be done? How does this impact other commitments, appointments, time, financial and other resources? Think about any conflict of interest issue. If you commit to A with one person and commit to B with another person and then A and B are in conflict with each other, you have a conflict of interest that you must resolve. How much time will it require and in what time frame? What other commitments do you have for that same time frame?

The adage is true, "To get something done, ask a busy person." A busy person is a person who knows how to get things done, has the energy, the resources and will find the time. But a busy person can get overloaded. Be careful about taking on commitments that you will have great difficulty in keeping.

A person who makes commitments is the person who makes this a better world. If we are not willing to make commitments, we are just along for the ride. By carefully considering our commitments, we can make a difference. What commitment have **you** recently made that will make the world around you a better place to be and also bring honor and glory to God?

STUDY QUESTIONS

1. List at least five major commitments that you currently have.
2. Are you considering some new commitments? If so, what is the process you are following to determine whether to proceed?
3. Have you ended any commitments in the past two years? Why did you make this decision? 83

"If we claim to have fellowship with Him but yet walk in the darkness, we lie and do not live by the truth." 1 John 1:6

Five ingredients for a healthy diet: "Adequacy, balance, calorie control, moderation and variety." *Eat and Heal*

WHAT DO YOU CARE DEEPLY ABOUT?

Peter Drucker is recognized by many as the foremost management consultant of the past half-century. He wrote over fifty books and was still teaching and lecturing a few years ago at age 95 before he died. He asked managers of non-profit and for-profit organizations many questions but one of the most provocative questions was this: "What do you care deeply about?" He was asking managers what their passions were, what was really important to them. Drucker was prompting the managers to think deeply about significance. He was urging them to devote time and energy to what is important.

Bob Buford wrote the book "Time Out" in which he talked about his "one thing." He was suggesting that of all the things that pass through our day, there will be one thing that is more important than anything else. In your personal life, what is the "one thing" that is the most important, the thing about which everything else revolves. Buford added that, for him, it is "to serve God in ways of God's choosing." In the past 24 hours, what has been your "one thing?"

Think about these questions for yourself. "What do you care deeply about?" What is your "one thing" that is the center of what drives you each day? Can you defend it as something important, of lasting importance, other-person centered? Or is it centered on you and the items in life that bring only direct pleasure to you? What do YOU care deeply about? What is your "one thing?"

We would be wise in answering these questions if we follow the exhortation of Philippians 2:3-4: "Do nothing out of selfish ambition or vain conceit. Rather, in humility value others above ourselves, not looking to our own interests but each of you to the interests of the others."

This is not just a mental exercise instead of doing "real work." These basic questions should determine what your "real work" really is. Once that is clear, then the prioritized goals should dive into whatever is before us whether it is a paid job, volunteer work or our personal and family life. What are you being prompted to do?

STUDY QUESTIONS

1. What do you "care deeply about?" Write it out and read it often.
2. What is your "one thing?" Share it with others to see what they have to say.
3. Maybe this thought process has prompted you in yet another direction. What is that and what are you doing about it?

54

"The real winners in life are the people who look at every situation with an expectation that they can make it work or make it better." Barbara Fletcher

"Wisdom's instruction is to fear the LORD, and humility comes before honor." Proverbs 15:33

KNOWING WHAT DONE MEANS

A very successful company with a stellar reputation was once asked what their secret to success was. The response was interesting. The representative said it involves many things but central is the concept of "Knowing what done means before you start a project."

Knowing what done means before you start, what defines completion of a project, requires thinking through the project at the outset. Planning every significant detail must be done from several perspectives – project designers, resources, the end user (customer) and those who will do the work. Sometimes government regulations are also involved.

Regardless of the nature of a project, what are the essential elements?

1. In a few words, what are we setting out to do?
2. When completed, how will we and/or our organization be impacted?
3. What will a successful project accomplish? What will be different?
4. What will it take to reach completion in time, money, people, and other resources?
5. What major obstacles does such a project have?
6. What is the projected timeline? When must the project be completed?
7. Who will provide the needed leadership?

Knowing what we are setting out to do is good planning in life. In our planning we must remember the word of the Lord in Proverbs 19:21: "Many are the plans in a person's heart, but it is the Lord's purpose that prevails." Prayer that asks for what the Lord's will is in "knowing what done means" will guide us from the outset.

Knowing what done means in the expectations of others (customers, public, government) and your own expectations at the point at which everyone will consider the project completed is essential. This means thinking ahead about what others mean when they envision the project. A detailed document that anticipates the expectations of all involved is a good beginning but it means going beyond that to the intangibles that lead to good will. Architects build models of a building before construction starts. Car manufacturers build concept cars before building the actual car. What is expected that at least one party to the equation <u>assumes</u> will be included? At the same time, we cannot delay starting a project indefinitely because some unknowns exist. President Lincoln fired Gen. McClelland in the Civil War because he spent too much time planning and not enough in doing.

Ultimately, can the project accomplish the purpose for which it was intended? Once all the expectations are on the table, the project might not be feasible. Or it could mean that the cost or timeline for the project needs to be revised. Happy endings come from a careful examination of the end expectations when you begin. Know what done means before you start.

STUDY QUESTIONS

1. Think of something you helped to accomplish at home, work or church. How well was "what done means" thought through before it began?
2. Knowing what done means in advance could change the timetable or even the feasibility of doing something. Have you ever had to scrap a project before it began based on thinking it through before it started?
3. As you contemplate completing something important in your life, what are the two or three things that are likely to get the most consideration? Time, money, ability, impact on others, meaningfulness, contributions of others, design, ethics?

44A

IT'S WHAT YOU DO NEXT

It's what you do next that counts. While it is possible to over emphasize this to say that the past doesn't matter or that the long-term future will take care of itself, we cannot change the past and our next step needs to be in the right direction to influence the longer-term future. We can go back and soften our past or build upon it. We soften the harsh parts of our past by going back to say I'm sorry or otherwise make mends of what we have done. It is also true that the first step toward our long-term future is taken today. We won't be as likely to reach our long-term goals if we fritter away our present or take steps now that are contrary to our long-term aspirations.

So how do we decide what to do next? If there are matters in our past that have a major influence on our future, are there steps we can take today to correct the effects of that past? Avoid the temptation to try to change the facts or to minimize the past. The past might have been relatively free of sin but still one in which we did not trust God to guide our lives resulting in a fruitless or aimless period of time. Or maybe we followed God's will in every area but one in which we reserved the decision to be made according to our personal preferences. If our past involves sin for which we have not been forgiven, we need to ask for forgiveness. If others have mistreated us, it is time to forgive. If our past was a wandering away from God, now is the time to seek Him. If our past was God pleasing, now we can build on it.

We have a present and a future. Every step today should be one that contributes to the future that conforms to God's will. Pray to learn God's will and how God would have you proceed today in fulfilling that will. The will of God might not appear overnight or even this week. It will require more than one prayer in all likelihood. We must be patient. We must listen. God might speak to us through others. God's will is likely to utilize the talents and gifts God has already given to us.

We must see ourselves as made by God to be one of His children. Where we have self-concept problems we need to seek ways to correct them. If we have a weakness, we can seek the help of others as well as pray to God. We can help others only when we are healed. God made each of us as one of His children. Love God and those God created.

Unless we have a pretty clear picture of the future that God wants for us, it will be difficult to know what steps to take now. The words of Paul might be helpful here. In Philippians 3:13 we read, "But one thing I do; forgetting what is behind and straining toward what is ahead." Pray about this and examine your God given talents, your experience and what you have done well. Formulate a plan with specific goals. We project future strength from our present strength. <u>Then, it's what you do next that counts.</u>

STUDY QUESTIONS

1. Are there issues in your past for which you need to seek forgiveness? Are you able to fully face the future until you have done this?
2. What are you doing today that will contribute to the future that will please both God and you?
3. It's what you do next that counts. What are you going to do next?

287

"Train up a child in the way he should go and when he is old he will not depart from it." Proverbs 22:6

"If God is for us, who can be against us? He who did not spare His own Son, but gave Him up for us all – how will He not also, along with Him, graciously give us all things." Romans 8:31-32

"Whenever we lose a friend, a part of us goes also."

"As you get older you realize that no one has all the answers. It turns out that life is an exercise in living with the certainty of uncertainty." Jason Killar

CHAPTER THREE

WISDOM AND OUR BEHAVIOR

Showing Wisdom, Criticism, What You Can Get Away With, Thinking and Habits, Reasoning, Kindness, Having Fun, Cash, Cadillacs and Comfort, Listening, Knowing The Right Thing, Standing Up For What Is Right, Ethical Standards, Balance, Stretching Your Mind

ETHICAL STANDARDS

All of us have ethical standards. We are told by parents, teachers, preachers and sometimes by bosses that we should act ethically. But what does that mean? How can we determine what is ethical?

Ethical behavior is measured against some standard. Think about what standard you are using. Society provides some of the standard we are expected to apply. Much of the societal standard comes from the Bible. Matthew 7:12 tells us, "So in everything, do to others what you would have them do to you..." Luke 6:31 in the KJV turns it around for a little different meaning: "As ye would that men should do to you, do ye also to them likewise."

The best and most pervasive ethical standards are found in the Bible. Both the Old Testament and New Testament provide us with guides to ethical behavior. When we don't have the opportunity to check the concordance of our Bible, we could use a quick guide. One that was heard often a few years ago was WWJD, "what would Jesus do?" We can apply this to the issues we face as we go through our day. Of course, the better we know Jesus, the more reliable our conclusion will be. The more we read the Bible, the more we will understand the ethical standards provided there.

A good secular standard is the guide used by Rotary Clubs, International. They have what they call, the Four Way Test. It asks,

> Is it the truth?
> Is it fair to all concerned?
> Is it beneficial to all concerned?
> Will it build good will and better friendships?

Acting ethically means applying a standard of what constitutes good ethics. What is your standard?

STUDY QUESTIONS

1. Think about how the wording of Luke 6:31 above applies to how you govern your life.
2. Does the standard of the Rotary Clubs fit well with the ethical standards in the Bible?
3. How do you test each situation to determine what action for you would be ethical?

69

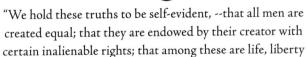

"We hold these truths to be self-evident, --that all men are created equal; that they are endowed by their creator with certain inalienable rights; that among these are life, liberty and the pursuit of happiness." President Thomas Jefferson

MAKING ETHICAL CHOICES

A choice is a decision to select between two or more alternatives or simply whether to take action on a given choice before us. An <u>ethical</u> choice is one in which the decision is based on an ethical standard. Not all choices are based on an ethical standard. We make many choices every day that are routine and not ethical in their foundation. Examples are whether we put on a green or a blue shirt or top today.

Ethical choices are based on some standard. Does that standard vary with the situation? Some would have us believe that all ethical decisions are based on the circumstances. However, as Christians we believe that ethical standards are stable and that the Holy Bible gives us that set of standards. The Ten Commandments are examples of biblical standards for ethical conduct. There are many others in the Bible. Some are highly specific while others cover a multitude of situations.

Covering a multitude of situations is Matthew 22 where Jesus reminds us that the greatest commandment is to "Love the Lord your God with all your heart and with all your soul and with all your mind" (Matthew 22:37). In Matthew 22:39 Jesus states: "And the second is like it: Love your neighbor as yourself."

Think about whether your major decisions have an ethical base. If so, what is the ethical standard that you apply? It might take courage to follow the ethical standards of the Bible but your conscience will not keep you awake if you do. As you face ethical decisions today, think about the biblical standards for the ethical choices you will make.

STUDY QUESTIONS

1. Think about a major decision you made that had ethical implications. How did you make your decision? Upon reflection now, do you think you made the right ethical choice?
2. Why are ethical choices difficult to make?
3. Describe the ethical standard you use for ethical choices.

3A

"For attaining wisdom and discipline; for understanding
words of insight, for acquiring a disciplined and prudent life,
doing what is right and just and fair; for giving prudence to
the simple, knowledge and discretion to the young – let the
wise listen and add to their learning, and let the discerning
get guidance –for understanding proverbs and parables,
the sayings and riddles of the wise." Proverbs 1:2-6

"Don't mistake politeness for a lack of strength." Sonya Sotomayer,
Current Justice of the United States Supreme Court

Dear friend, do not imitate what is evil but what is good." 3 John 11

ACHIEVING BALANCE

We face a number of balance issues in the utilization of time, energy, money and attention. Nothing in our lives can get all of our time, our energy, our money or our attention. At the same time, we cannot live such simple lives that there would be only one aspect of our lives. A juggler can keep one or more balls in the air. In our lives we decide how many balls <u>we want</u> to keep in the air. How complex do we want our lives to be? We decide from each of the balls we put in the air how we will distribute our time, our energy, our money and our attention (focus) on each. Our decisions about balance are a reflection of our faith and the rest of our values.

The first to get our time, our energy, our money and our attention is self. Not to the extent of being selfish (self-centered) but each of us must be healthy (physically and emotionally), have normal or better energy and have some earnings before we can help others. If we do not care for ourselves, we are not in a position to help anyone else or to keep any balls in the air.

Second, we need to meet our commitments to God, then family and then others. What are these commitments and how much of our time, energy, time and commitment (focus) does each require? We can look at the life of Jesus to see how he balanced his time and energy. He was never in excess and never inadequate on anything he talked about or did. This should be our goal as well.

Part of our balance needs to include God's plan for service to others including family and friends. To be a servant leader, we should look for opportunities to serve others. We are told that when we <u>should</u> act but fail to act, it is a sin (James 4:17). Our best service will utilize our God given gifts, our education and talents.

Most of us have some special interests and we will be tempted to devote a great amount of our time to that endeavor at the expense of our obligations. When we pursue our special interests in our leisure time and with our disposable income, it can bring pleasure to our lives and maybe even to others around us. However, temptation can lead to excess and thus place this activity out of balance with the rest of our life.

Prayer and Bible reading are likely to be activities that don't get enough of our time. We spend 24 hours every day and we have a responsibility for basic care of ourselves and then seek balance in everything else. Think of ways that you can achieve balance in your life emphasizing worship of God and helping others today.

STUDY QUESTIONS

1. Think of two aspects of your life in which you must achieve balance. How do you do it?
2. Are you the type of person who likes to keep many balls in the air with a complex life or do you prefer one ball in the air and a simpler life? Why?
3. How do you know which type of person God wants you to be? 4A

When we say or do too much or too little, we are out of balance. The optimum achievement comes when we find balance in the many aspects of our lives and do so continually. Anonymous

WHAT ARE YOU A SLAVE TO?

What are we slaves to in our daily lives? The Apostle Peter, writing in 2 Peter 2:19, is talking about people who seek to deceive others. The text reads, "They promise them freedom, while they themselves are slaves of depravity – for a man is slave to whatever has mastered him."

We can be a slave to depravity like the people Peter was describing or we can elect another choice. Some people like to think of themselves as free spirits letting the wind guide them like the chaff blowing off the field. These free spirits are never really free, however, because they still have strong preferences, some of which are the things they dislike causing them to be opposed to societal norms. Some of us are slaves to our work by devoting all of our negotiable time to our careers and accomplishing work goals. Some of us are devoted to our play, thinking that the ideal life is to sit on a beach to enjoy the water and the freedom to pursue what we consider fun. Still others of us enjoy doing as little as possible, maybe using the television to entertain us.

We might enjoy being a free spirit at times and those of us fortunate enough to have a job certainly want to do our best at work. There is much to be said about leisure time and having fun and sometimes we just need to rest. We should seek a balance among these pursuits.

Being a slave to something means to do whatever that force causes you to think, say and do. For the committed Christian, our devotion is to God seeking to follow His commandments and to bring honor and glory to Him. The really neat thing about this is that we can have it all. While being devoted to God, we are free – free from sin and depravity and having multiple choices in life while remaining true to our Christian faith commitment. We can work hard in our job. In fact, the Bible directs us to do our best in whatever we do. We can engage in fun and leisure. Due to our commitment to God, we can take this to the next level by serving others and focusing on their needs.

So what are you a slave to? What has mastered you? If it were depravity you might not be reading this. But you might be a slave to your own personal needs and desires. Try a commitment to God and enjoy your life while serving others.

STUDY QUESTIONS

1. Which of the types described best fits you?
2. Make a list of all the things that control your time and effort each day.
3. Analyze the list, separating out those items that are there because you put them there (short term and long term). Is there anything left?

112

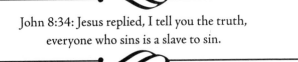

John 8:34: Jesus replied, I tell you the truth, everyone who sins is a slave to sin.

EXERCISING DISCIPLINE

When we think of discipline we tend to think first about disciplining children to make them behave in the manner we desire. But we are talking about disciplining ourselves. Our own behavior needs as much disciplining as that of a child. There are some differences. Our behavior is more pervasive – it will affect more people and in more serious ways. Second, there are few people who are there to discipline us. When we act inappropriately at work our supervisor might step in. When we act illegally a police officer will act when the police officer sees our illegal action. But most of the time our behavior is between God and us. Remember that behavior includes not only what we do but also what we think and say.

God gave us the Holy Spirit to help us in what we do, think and say. One of the roles of the Holy Spirit in our lives is to help us be disciplined: "For the Spirit God gave us does not make us timid, but gives us power, love and self-discipline" (II Timothy 1:7).

Self-discipline is not just about bad behavior. It is also about wasted behavior or senseless behavior. Discipline could be used to push us into good behavior for which we lack the motivation. It could be behavior in which we are the primary one affected (such as staying on a diet). For most of us it is a matter of sticking to our goals. If you have no goals in life other than to be alive tomorrow, then there is not much to discipline except for how you are affecting others. But let's assume that you do have some goals and you are serious about achieving them.

To exercise self-discipline, it is important to set goals that are measurable, realistic and understandable. First, it is important to have goals that can be measured as to the extent to which they have been achieved. A goal that says this year I am going to make the world a better place is difficult to evaluate at the end of the year as to whether you accomplished that goal. Rationalization can help us to think that a very general goal has been reached when, if fact, you don't really know whether it was reached or not. Second, goals must be realistic while at the same time ones that will stretch you beyond what is easily done. Realistic means attainable under the best of circumstances and with the best possible effort. Third, goals have to be understandable. If at the end of the period (such as a year) you cannot quite comprehend what you had in mind when you wrote the goal, the goal was not written to be understood and not likely attainable.

Self-discipline comes in when you monitor your behavior to ensure that you are on target. It can't be done just at the end. It has to be constant just as driving a car requires that at every moment you are keeping the car on the road and stopping when necessary. Self-discipline will require adjusting behavior as you go along. Self-discipline can be assisted by being accountable to another person who is aware of your goals and will talk with you about their perceptions of your progress. For self-discipline to work, you must really want to achieve the goal. Write some goals that meet the above criteria and then discipline yourself to attain the goals. <u>You</u> will be winner.

STUDY QUESTIONS

1. Reflect on these two statements from the article: "But most of the time our behavior is between God and us. Remember that behavior includes not only what we do but also what we think and say."
2. What would it mean to be "accountable to another person?"
3. If you were to exercise self-discipline every day effectively, what personal faults might you overcome?

5

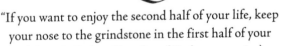

"If you want to enjoy the second half of your life, keep your nose to the grindstone in the first half of your life." B. C. Forbes (founder of Forbes magazine)

"Democracy does not contain any force that will check the constant tendency to put more and more on the public payroll. The state is like a hive of bees in which the drones display, multiply and starve the workers so the idlers will consume the food and the workers will perish." Plato (427-347 BC)

COMMON COURTESIES

As we grow up and mature we are taught a number of common courtesies that will facilitate healthy and pleasant relationships with other people. Our parents, our mothers in particular, will work on these with us during the growing up years. Sometimes we rebel from them or we forget to practice them. In school many of these common courtesies are reinforced.

Here are some of them:

1. Wash your hands before preparing or eating food.
2. Take off your hat (men and boys) when you enter a building.
3. Hold the door for others.
4. Greet other people as you encounter them. Say "hello."
5. Never tell a lie.
6. Speak only when appropriate.
7. Think before you speak – say only what you intended to say.
8. Don't take what isn't yours. Put things back where you found them.
9. When a line forms for something we want, go to the end of the line.
10. Help other people who are in need whenever possible.
11. Stand up and remove your caps for singing the National Anthem.
12. Close your eyes when you pray.
13. Don't take the last available helping at the dinner table.
14. Say "Yes, Sir" and "Yes, Maam", when speaking to others, particularly your elders.
15. Do to others what you would like for them to do for you.
16. Be kind in what you say and don't gossip.
17. Demonstrate an interest in other people.
18. Drive safely; be courteous to other drivers.
19. Look out for danger which might affect others.
20. Smile when you make eye contact with others.

How many of these have you done already today or this week? What would you like to add to the list?

And last, we need to heed the exhortation of the Apostle Peter in I Peter 3:8-9: "Finally, all of you, be like-minded, sympathetic, love one another, be compassionate and humble. Do not repay evil with evil or insult with insult. On the contrary, repay evil with blessing, because to this you were called so that you may inherit a blessing."

STUDY QUESTIONS

1. Is there one of these that is difficult for you to do? Why is that?
2. Why do we remove hats and stand up for the National Anthem?
3. What is the effect of a smile?

64

"Love is a choice we make." "When you love you're acting the most like Jesus." "The person who loves, wins." Pastor Dr. Charles Stanley

"Courtesies extended are sometimes returned but the joy of extending it is always present." Anonymous

LISTENING

Dr. Charles Stanley once made the comment that "Being willing to listen to others is godly." He added, "When you turn a deaf ear, you will likely be deaf to God's will for you." Further, "When you are willing to listen, God will give you the gift of discernment showing you what to listen to." Proverbs 1:5 tells us, "...let the wise listen and add to their learning, and let the discerning get guidance."

In order to listen, we must first set aside whatever has our attention. Some people talk about their ability to "multi-task" but this really means in most cases that the individual is able to quickly move from one item to another and then back again much like a good cook does when preparing a many course meal. Our sub conscience will help us in being able to do multiple routine things at the same time but not particularly well. Some people like to text while they are driving but their driving quality is not acceptable while texting. The human mind handles one major thing at a time well (Einstein's biographer said he could handle two) while being mindful of others. Effective listening requires that it be the major thing getting the attention of our mind.

Listening to someone else speak or reading what they have written, we must discern the difference between what we heard them say and what they intended to say. There is always some difference. When we don't choose our words carefully or let random thoughts escape without the filter of thinking about the words we communicate, something other than what we intended is received regardless of how well the recipient knows us. When listening we are apt to form quick conclusions about what a person is saying before we hear (or see, if reading) all of the words. That will cause communication to suffer as well.

For most of us listening to God is difficult. To begin with, we must be still without competing sounds for our major attention. Second, we have to wait on God, to listen on His schedule. Third, we have to apply what we think we have heard in a manner that is consistent with the nature of God's love and will for us.

Inattentive listening leads to frustration and poor communication which leads to misunderstandings. To avoid misunderstandings, we must try harder to hear what other people are saying and meaning in order to accomplish good communication. When we stop listening, we cease to grow in wisdom. All of us want others to listen to us. It is a courtesy to listen to others and listening carefully has clear benefits for us. When listening to God we must give our full attention and be patient for God's timing. If we set aside a time for prayer and listening for God's response, we will be closer to God and more likely to hear God's message for us.

STUDY QUESTIONS

1. Are you a good listener? What might you do to improve your listening to others?
2. If others are not listening well to you, how do you react? We could get angry but if we make another try, the listener might hear.
3. How well do you listen to God? What could you do to improve this? 177A

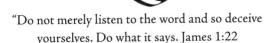

"Do not merely listen to the word and so deceive yourselves. Do what it says. James 1:22

"The first duty of love is to listen." Theologian Paul Tillich

ARE YOU A BULLY?

Are you a bully? My guess is that few people who act as a bully would admit to being one and would explain their behavior in some way that they think makes it acceptable. The dictionary defines bully "as the use of force, threat or coercion to abuse, intimidate or aggressively dominate others."

We tend to think of a bully as some kid at school who is bigger than the others who threatens and intimidates other kids. But probably most bullies are adults. Anger has the capacity to cause us to behave as a bully. Examples of ways an adult acts as a bully is when a person: 1) rushes in to take a parking place ahead of another person heading for it, 2) cuts in line (often with a car), 3) tailgates another car to intimidate the other driver to go faster, 4) dominates a conversation in order to draw attention to self, 5) ignores or snubs people they consider inferior, and 6) puts down others in a conversation and other instances. You can think of other situations in which someone being a bully is frustrating to you.

There is a difference between being a **bully**, being **aggressive**, being **assertive** and being **self-confident**. There is never a time when being a bully is appropriate. A bully acts without regard for the rights of others. There are times when being aggressive might be appropriate such in the defense of our rights. Being assertive means acting proactively but within the bounds of the rights of others. Proactive or assertive people are those who get things done. All of us should be self-confident meaning that we are confident without being arrogant and with high regard for others. A confident person is capable of being other person centered. A bully, on the other hand, is likely to be acting from a lack of self-confidence.

There is no positive reference to being a bully in the Bible. There are references in which being a bully is looked down upon such as John 9:28, 18:26 and Mt 9:24. The ultimate case of bullying was the stoning of Stephen (Acts 7:54-60). When you see a person being a bully or a bully attacks you, do you have the courage to confront the bully? Have you ever acted like any of the bully examples above? Pray that you will be able to say no, I am not a bully.

STUDY QUESTIONS

1. How often do you see an adult acting as a bully? Think of the examples of lack of courtesy and the way that we see people drive.
2. The more self-confident you are, the less likely someone will attempt to bully you. Are you likely to be bullied?
3. Read the Scriptures that are cited above. Are Christians likely to be bullied today?

311

"We are what we habitually do." Aristotle (384-322 B C)

"The Proverbs of Solomon: A wise son brings joy to his father, but a foolish son brings grief to his mother." Proverbs 10:1

"Mockers resent correction, so they avoid the wise." Proverbs 15:12

"Our greatest weakness is not an enemy from without but one from within. Our own weak wills cause us to stumble. But Jesus Christ frees us from the foolishness of sin and the weakness in ourselves." Pastor Ravi Zacharias

CASH, CADILLACS AND COMFORT

In one of his sermons, Dr. Adrian Rogers said that we tend to seek the three C's, cash, Cadillacs and comfort. Each of us <u>needs</u> some cash, a dependable form of transportation and some comfort. Dr. Rogers was pointing out that when these three C's become our priorities one, two and three in life, we are being shortsighted. All three will perish when we die or when the Second Coming takes place, whichever comes first.

We need cash to pay for the essentials in life, food, shelter and personal care. The problem can come when we are obsessed with getting more cash in order to have more and better food, a nicer place (or places) to stay and greater personal comfort. When we put money first in our priorities in life, we are prone to seek the easiest ways to accumulate the greatest amount. This could mean that which is illegal or unethical which we explain as "the end justifies the means" or "the early bird gets the worm." Jesus did not condemn having cash or even lots of it. When talking to the rich young ruler he told him to give it away but it was not for the purpose of the ruler not having his riches, it was a test to see whether the money or salvation was priority number one in his life. Having cash is a worthy priority as long as it is not priority number one.

Dr. Rogers mentioned Cadillacs as another of the three C's that we tend to want. Most of us need transportation and, if we have the cash, we can buy a Cadillac or some other form of luxury transportation. There is nothing wrong in wanting to own a Cadillac unless that priority ranks higher than seeking God.

The third item listed by Dr. Rogers in his three C's of cash, Cadillacs and comfort, could lead us to avoid work, being lazy and being self-centered. We should all seek basic comfort and health care but when it is a priority above our salvation, we are thinking only of ourselves in our present life and not of the future. Earthly comforts will cease when we die, salvation continues forever.

The basic conclusion of this is that we can seek cash, Cadillacs and comfort as long as they are no higher in our priorities than two, three and four with number one being seeking God, accepting Jesus as our savior and living the life that the Bible teaches us to live. That is a big number one. However, when it is number one in our priorities, look at what happens to our desire for cash, Cadillacs and comfort. Much of our cash becomes support for our Church and other ministries rather than just for ourselves and those around us. We might still have a Cadillac or some other nice car, but our last dollar does not go for that car. We might still live in a very nice house but should not if that house means we cannot afford to support our Church and other ministries. When we consider support of our church and other ministries, the words of Jesus must become our guiding principle in all of these things. He said, as quoted in Matthew 6:33: "But seek first His (God's) kingdom and His (God's) righteousness and all these things (cash, Cadillacs, comfort) will be given to you as well."

So what is priority number one in your life? God is the only priority that yields rewards in both this life and the next. All other priorities in whatever our three C's might be will end in this lifetime and could prevent us from making God our number one priority. Making God first requires that we place God above self in our priorities. What are the first five priorities in your life?

STUDY QUESTIONS

1. What are your first five priorities in life? Is God number one?
2. Why did Jesus say it was difficult for a rich man to enter Heaven?
3. How much cash do you need, how nice of a car is essential for you and how do you define adequate comfort? Do any of your answers make it difficult to support your Church and other ministries?

334

AN ACT OF KINDNESS

Aesop 620-564 BC, original writer of Aesop's Fables, wrote, "An act of kindness, however small, is never wasted." Kindness is a favorable and supportive attitude toward a person or object. Because attitudes are one of the parts of us that we control, we all have the opportunity to exhibit kindness. Kindness, however, requires that the person showing this attitude be one who is not wrapped up in self but rather has an abiding interest in the welfare of others as well as objects.

An act of kindness must be based in what will benefit another person, place or thing and not based solely on what **we** want to do for or to that person, place or thing. The focus must be on meeting needs and providing benefits for others and not what is particularly meaningful to us. Of course, needs and benefits must be based on real and not imagined or ill-conceived desires. An ill-conceived desire could be an alcoholic who wants an alcoholic drink. It would not be an act of kindness to meet that desire. There are times when we must help others to define what their needs and desires are and the manner in which we might help to meet that need including its timing, possible cost and impact on others.

Kindness is most appreciated when the recipient recognizes that the person or group offering the kindness is providing the kindness out of a desire to help rather than a sense of duty or compulsion. This recognition can be shown with a smile and with going beyond the basic necessity of the situation such as not only helping a person who has fallen but also seeing them to a place of safety and stability. A smile indicates a concern and interest in the person receiving the kindness.

We are never too young to learn the value of kindness. An attitude of kindness developed at an early age is a wonderful attribute to nourish the rest of our lives. It can come from kind and loving parents and other adult role models including teachers, friends and church members. When we choose our friends who have the qualities we admire, we are more likely to develop those qualities ourselves. A dear friend named Bill, who has now gone on to Heaven, was a friend from the days when we were in the high school band together. He was always kind toward others with nary an unkind word. When you met his Mother you could understand where the quality of kindness began with him. We can have this same kind of influence with children who enter our lives.

Theologian R. C. Sproul links kindness to patience in mentioning Galatians 5 which lists the "works of the flesh." None of them involve kindness. But when we look at the "fruit of the Spirit," we find "love, joy, peace, forbearance, kindness, goodness, faithfulness, gentleness, and self-control." Each of these is manifested through kindness. In verse 25 Paul tells us, "Since we live by the Spirit, let us keep in step with the Spirit." That means that if we call ourselves Christian, we must show kindness in how we express each of the characteristics just mentioned.

There is also a relationship between kindness and humility. Humility allows us to concentrate on others instead of self. When we are comfortable in our humility, we will not concentrate on how to elevate ourselves. Instead, we can demonstrate acts of kindness toward others.

When we show kindness, <u>we</u> benefit as well. When we make others happy, we are likely to be happy ourselves. Further, when we are kind to others, we are more likely to be kind to ourselves. A person who does not like the person he or she has become is likely to be critical of self and critical of others. When we are kind to ourselves, we are more likely to build on positive attributes. Positive leads to positive. If we are kind to the person we have become, we are likely to be kind to others. Are you kind to yourself so that you can in turn be kind to others?

STUDY QUESTIONS

1. Think about your humility. Do you have sufficient humility so that you are able to concentrate on being kind to others?
2. Are you kind to yourself or do you repeatedly put yourself down? God created you in His image and wants the best for you.
3. Think of a recent act of kindness on your part. What motivated you to be kind? Was it a sense of duty or other compulsion or was it an act of love that prompted the kindness?

414

WHAT WE CAN GET AWAY WITH

Most of us think of ourselves as persons who obey the laws and we do what God tells us to do as set forth in the Bible. We haven't done anything like what is portrayed on the television news and God hasn't spoken to us to tell us of some sin. In fact, our conscience is quite clear. We are happy with ourselves and what we are doing.

Think about the last time you were driving on the Interstate. Did you drive according to the speed limit or did you set your speed at what you thought you could get away with? When the light turned yellow, did you come to a stop or did you rationalize that you can make it through the light before the other cars start to move? The last time you came to a stop sign, did you make a real stop or just glide through when you saw there was no other traffic? Did you need a ream of paper at home so you picked one up at work and brought it home? Did you share information with someone but you left out a few things that you didn't want to tell because you thought that person would never know the difference? When you sold a used car, maybe traded it in, how much did you share when asked what problems the car had? Did you tell your spouse the whole story about what you spent after visiting your favorite store?

We are tempted to go through life thinking we are fine, upstanding citizens when, in fact, <u>we make many decisions based on what we think we can get away with in our actions.</u> Not speeding on the Interstate, making a full stop at the stop or stopping right away when the traffic light turns yellow, will cost us some time and energy. We can rationalize that there are other things in life that are so much more important that our time and energy needs to be placed there. We can rationalize that life is short so we need to make the best of the time we have. We might even rationalize that we are so important that the people we might have offended will get over it and my importance justifies my actions.

Your reaction at this point might be either to be offended with these questions being asked of you or maybe your conscience is pricked just a little. Maybe it has caused you to recall the person who sounded a horn at you when you ran the red light or missed the stop sign. If you are offended by the questions, there isn't much that this message can do for you. But if your conscience tells you that possibly I need to change some of my behaviors, then think about slowing down a little to "smell the roses," to think primarily about the needs and wants of others, to think about what is really important in my life. Taking a chance by driving through on a yellow light isn't worth it when you consider what might happen. Read James 4:17 about the sin of not doing something that we know we should do.

The basic message here is to advocate thinking about what is really important in life. Your salvation is of utmost importance. After that your goals and your relationships with others need to be high on your list. Then think about those areas of your life where your actions might be guided by "what I can get away with." What corrections will you make?

STUDY QUESTIONS

1. Of the situations mentioned above, is there one that applies to you? Which one(s)?
2. There is a difference between doing the right thing or the best choice in a given set of circumstances and doing what you can get away with. Think of a situation in which you rationalized and didn't do the right thing or make the best choice.
3. How can you program yourself to avoid making decisions based on what you can get away with?

253

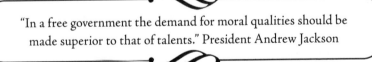

"In a free government the demand for moral qualities should be made superior to that of talents." President Andrew Jackson

MARK TWAIN #1

Drawing from the wisdom of Mark Twain, we find this statement: "Always do right. This will gratify some people, and astonish the rest."

Let's look at the first sentence. The principle is "Always do right." It does not say do right when convenient or when personally profitable. "Always" is a very pervasive word. It does not allow for exceptions.

The second word is "do" which is an action, not just thinking about the right thing to do, but also taking action. This is different from watching or urging someone else to take action. It suggests that action be taken whenever appropriate by you, by me.

Then consider what "right" means. What is "right?" To "do right" requires some standard to determine whether an action is right or not, that is, applied as opposed to whim or the flipping of a coin. "Right" is not based on chance. "Right cannot be based on our decision about what we <u>think</u> is right or wrong motivated by self-interest. Nor should the standard be the behavior of those around us. But Christians are committed to following the teachings in the Bible. You might argue that not all life situations are specifically covered in the Bible. However, the Bible has many broad statements such as in the Ten Commandments and the words of the Apostle John:

> Do not love the world or anything in the world. If anyone loves the world, love for the Father is not in them. For everything in the world – the lust of the flesh, the lust of the eyes, and the pride of life – comes not from the Father but from the world. The world and its desires pass away, but whoever does the will of God lives forever (1 John 2:15-17).

If we are weak in our faith, we are likely to use those around us as a standard instead of the Christian standard found in the Bible.

Mark Twain mentioned that doing right will "gratify some people and astonish the rest." Those who also accept the Christian standard (even if not

115

Christians) understand that this standard is best for society as a whole and thus generally for all of us. For those who live by a different standard, the person or group might be astonished or critical of the stand we have taken. Criticism for doing the right thing is common in our society. Each of us must determine whether we are strong enough to stand up to the criticism.

There are gray areas, to be sure, when two Christians might disagree with each claiming to be following a teaching in the Bible. Christians have divided over this for hundreds of years. However, we must be alert to when the Bible is claimed to support a view already held by an individual or group. The Bible must be taken as a whole rather than a verse taken out of context. When our interpretation of the Bible is far from other believers on one or more points, that should tell us to dig deeper and more broadly in the Scripture before continuing in our conclusions.

The Bible is the standard that always sets a positive standard. Even for those who are not Christians, the Bible sets a standard of what is "good." For Christians, it provides a standard of what is "good" that we must follow if we continue to claim that we are Christians. Let us continue to "gratify some," as Mark Twain put it, and "astonish others." Will you follow the maxim of Mark Twain to "Always do good?" What is your standard of what is "good?"

STUDY QUESTIONS

1. What does the word "always" mean to you?
2. When you make decisions about what to do, how do you determine what is right?
3. How do the forces of "politically correct" and "socially correct" intimidate you?

31A

MARK TWAIN #2

In the last program we introduced the comment by Mark Twain who has been quoted as saying, "Always do right. This will gratify some people, and astonish the rest."

We talked about the principle. Let us think about the application of the principle. First, he says it "will gratify some people." These are the people whose values agree with your values, your sense of what is right. Hopefully, your sense of what is right is in agreement with Christian principles even if you are not a Christian.

Some people will not be gratified by your sense of what is "right." Remember Mark Twain's comment that "This will gratify some people, and astonish the rest." What did he mean by "astonish the rest?" Those who have a different standard of what is "right" might be surprised and even angered by your stand for what is "right." This can be the test of whether you really stand behind your sense of what is "right." If you back off from a position due to opposition, it is not a position you really held – just one you knew about.

Some people determine what is right based on what they think is good for themselves at the moment. Their thinking is that if it feels good, it must be right. This type of thinking is tempting to all of us but it is not a useful standard. What feels good at the moment could be a disaster for us in the long term.

To adhere to a standard that will "astonish the rest," we must turn to the Bible. The importance of the Bible in our lives is expressed by the Psalmist in Psalm 119:105: "Your word is a lamp for my feet, a light on my path." But the Bible will not be a "lamp for my feet" unless we read the Bible on a regular basis.

Are you a Christian following the biblical standard or are you just claiming to be a Christian following a different standard? The same biblical standard must be followed in all situations and at all times, not just when it is convenient. God watches over our every move and we should watchful over what we do as well.

STUDY QUESTIONS

1. Look up Mark Twain. Who was he?
2. Are you following the Bible or "just claiming to be a Christian?"
3. How do you determine what is right?

32

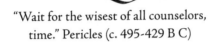

"Wait for the wisest of all counselors,
time." Pericles (c. 495-429 B C)

"It takes a wise man to recognize a wise man."
Xenophanes (c. 570 – c. 475 B C)

"The Lord is my strength and my shield; my heart
trusts in Him, and He helps me. My heart leaps for
joy, and with my song I praise Him." Psalm 28:7

SIDNEY POTIER'S ADVICE

Sidney Potier, the first African-American actor to win an Academy Award, in a TV interview was asked for advice he would give to other people today. He said get an education. Second, he said, "be articulate with words." Being articulate will "give flight to your dreams."

Let's look at those two goals. Getting an education can apply to a person of any age. It changes our self-perception by challenging our current worldview. When we see ourselves as capable of things that yesterday were beyond our thinking, we can consider doing those things. Education also opens doors with others who consider a high school diploma or a college degree as entry points for discussion. Education also puts us in contact with other like-minded people who might challenge and motivate us to reach goals we would not have considered on our own.

The second piece of advice from Sidney Potier was to "be articulate with words. Being articulate with words will give flight to your dreams." In order to be articulate, it is first essential that thoughts are clear in our mind. The clearer it is in our mind, the easier it is to be articulate in describing those thoughts. To be articulate we must train ourselves to use vocabulary that will be readily understood and yet the most precise words for the thought we are attempting to communicate.

Being articulate means to be able to say more accurately what is on our mind. If a thought is not clear in our brain, it won't be clear when we try to explain it to others. If we can think of an idea and then articulate it, it moves much closer to having an impact. Clarity of thought is helped by the setting which must be conducive to effective communication with a minimum of distracting interference. The more we make an effort at being articulate, the more articulate we are likely to become. Reading articulate writers and hearing articulate speakers will give us further enhancement in this skill. Talking and writing will help in being articulate as we listen to ourselves and detect whether we are being understood. Mastery of the language will help discover words that more adequately express thoughts. Speaking or writing deliberately will increase the force of your words.

Education and being articulate go together. They help to make us a more effective person. How might you apply Potier's advice in these two areas of your life?

STUDY QUESTIONS

1. Look up the history of Sidney Potier to see how he has been a role model.
2. How closely related are a good education and being articulate?
3. Evaluate how articulate you are. Do people understand you clearly?

39

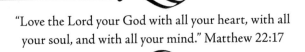

"Love the Lord your God with all your heart, with all your soul, and with all your mind." Matthew 22:17

THE IDEAL FRIEND

Most of us get great enjoyment from our friends. We have fun together. We do enjoyable things together. We support each other when needed. It's good to know we have friends to turn to in both good times and the times of disappointment. So what is the nature of this friend?

First, he or she loves God just as you do. This means you start with a similar value system. You value many of the same things such as kindness, love, respect as well as having fun and enjoying this wonderful earth God created for us. We would want that friend to know John 14:6, where Jesus is recorded saying, "I am the way and the truth and the life" so that he or she accepts that salvation comes only through Jesus Christ.

Second, this friend has a healthy self-concept. This is evident in that they meet most of their own needs without being dependent on others for emotional support. Because they have a healthy self-concept they are able to focus on things outside of themselves.

Third, this friend is other-person centered. Once his or her basic needs are met, he or she will devote time and energy to making the world a better place for other people. This will be evident in everything that he or she says (orally or written), thinks and does.

Fourth, this friend will be honest, a friend through all the trials of life, generous with time and money, full of empathy for others, willing to reach out to others in need, a volunteer in the church or other parts of the community, willing to be a leader and to take on responsibilities when appropriate and finds the best in others through encouragement and support.

Fifth, this friend is loving and capable of showing that love toward others making it evident that the love is sincere. Love means caring about the other person passionately, wanting the very best for the person being loved.

Sixth, this friend has a focus in life guided by goals and making progress on those goals. While working on the goals, this friend is able to find a balance in life between work and relaxation, duty and allowing others to lead, needs of self and the needs of others.

How many friends like this do you have? Now the test. It's time for you to <u>be</u> this friend to someone who needs a friend. Go out and be this friend for someone.

STUDY QUESTIONS

1. How many friends do you have who meet the criteria suggested above?
2. How close do you come to fitting the criteria in extending friendship to others?
3. If there are two or three of the criteria where you recognize that you need to improve, what are they and what is your plan for addressing these characteristics? 166

"Friends don't count in fair weather. It is when troubles come that friends count." President Harry S. Truman

Dr. Warren Bennis (former President of UCLA):
Excellence is a better teacher than mediocrity. The lessons of the ordinary are everywhere. Truly profound and original insights are to be found only in studying the exemplary.

LET US REASON TOGETHER

The media tells us we are a divided nation even though most of us live in our part of the world in which most people are similar to us in faith and outlook on life. Yet there are many others who don't relate to God or see the world like we do. We can dismiss the others as being wrong or we can say LET US REASON TOGETHER. Emotion has its place when we feel strongly about what we have reasoned together. Making wise decisions, however, must be made on the basis of facts, values (including our faith) and reason. When we reject reason, we have only the options of silence or rebellion as in a demonstration.

As Isaiah was working with a rebellious nation, he pleaded with them. The wording in the King James Version of Isaiah 1:18-19 reads:

> Come now, and let us <u>reason</u> together, saith the Lord: Though your sins be as scarlet, they shall be as white as snow; though they be red like crimson, they shall be as wool. If ye be willing and obedient, ye shall eat the good of the land.

To reason with others is to explain or justify an action or event of the past, present or future. Webster says "It reflects the power of the mind to think, understand and form judgments by a process of logic." Isaiah was attempting to persuade God's people to come to their senses and return to Godly ways. But not all attempts at reasoning succeed.

Thomas Jefferson said: "In a republican nation whose citizens are to be led by <u>reason</u> and persuasion and not by force, the art of reasoning becomes of first importance." So in a representative democracy as we have in the United States, Canada and many other parts of the world, we attempt to make decisions by persuasion rather than force. When decisions are made by force, there is often no victor. Through persuasion we can work together to build and create by utilizing the ideas and talents of many people to build that which is greater than any one person could create.

Jesus used reason in his thinking. John 12:27 reads: "Now my soul in troubled, and what shall I say? Father, save me from this hour? No, it was for this very <u>reason</u> I came to this hour. Father, glorify your name!" While it was physically attractive to avoid the agony of the cross, Jesus prevailed with the reason for his appearance on earth.

John 15 records an episode in which reason did not prevail. "If the world hates you, keep in mind that it hated me first. If you belonged to the world, it would love you as its own. As it is, you do not belong to the world, but I have chosen you out of the world. That is why the world hates you" (15:18-19). Jesus concludes in verse 25 with "But this is to fulfill what is written in their Law: 'They hated me <u>without reason.</u>'"

Peter gives advice to the early church: "But in your hearts revere Christ as Lord. Always be prepared to give an answer to everyone who asks you to give the <u>reason</u> for the hope that you have" (I Peter 3:15). In 2 Peter 1:3-7 we read:

> His divine power has given us everything we need for a godly life through our knowledge of Him who called us by His own glory and goodness. Through these he has given us his very great and precious promises, so that through them you might participate in the divine nature, have escaped the corruption in the world caused by evil desires. For this very <u>reason,</u> make every effort to add to your faith goodness; and to goodness, knowledge; and to knowledge, self-control; and to self-control, perseverance; and to perseverance, godliness; and to godliness, mutual affection; and to mutual affection, love.

In the United States and other republics, we encourage people to state their difference even to the extent of demonstrating in the streets. But reason seldom prevails in the street. Let <u>us</u> reason together as in these passages from the Bible to understand and apply the great opportunity for us to reason together, without compromising our faith, to reach the best possible decisions for our country.

THINKING

Let's explore what it means to think. Albert Einstein said, "Education is not the learning of facts, it is the training of the mind to think." Einstein was not talking about acting on impulse, habit or training. He was considering a higher level of thinking when the human mind reflects upon significance, cause and effect, relationships between ideas, why things are as they are and how to effect change that would be positive for the future. Higher-level thinking is considering the <u>why</u> question more than the what question. In order to consider <u>why</u>, it is true that there must already be some answering of the <u>what</u> issue. We need knowledge before we can begin to think about that knowledge and how to take that knowledge to the next level.

Human beings tend to stay away from higher level thinking through accepting what they have been told or thought they have been told, through seeking simple solutions to complex issues without considering the complexity, through seeking the path of least resistance and the least amount of work. Human needs are in a hierarchy with food, water and shelter the most basic. When we are concerned with how to meet needs at the basic level, there is little opportunity for higher-level thinking. But most of us are not at this subsistence level much of the time. We have the opportunity to engage in higher-level thinking but seldom do.

The Bible directs us to think. The Apostle Paul in Philippians 4:8 told us: "Finally, brothers and sisters, whatever is true, whatever is noble, whatever is right, whatever is pure, what ever is lovely, whatever is admirable – if anything is excellent or praiseworthy – think about such things."

An anonymous writer once said, "Take care of your thoughts when you are alone and take care of your words when you are with people." Our thoughts when we are alone are often just daydreaming when we allow our mind to float from one scene to another without any intentional thought process. But our thoughts <u>can</u> be intentional and they <u>can</u> be on a higher plane if we make that choice.

Thinking on a higher level does not require high intelligence. In fact, Albert Einstein once said, "Everybody is a genius. But if you judge a fish by its ability to climb a tree, it will live its whole life believing it is stupid." Each of us is unique. Most of us are capable of higher-level thinking. Rather than just accepting information about how something works, ask about why it works, why it is there and why it can't or does not go beyond its present capabilities. Think about significance, cause and effect, relationships between ideas and how to effect positive change. Do some higher level thinking about yourself and God's role for you.

STUDY QUESTIONS

1. Identify a topic on which you have engaged in higher-level thinking.
2. What did this higher-level thinking lead you to, what conclusions did you reach?
3. Think about your relationship with God. 185

"It is through your mind that God reaches you." "The mind is the battle ground." Pastor Dr. Adrian Rogers

"A wise man hears one word and understands two." Hebrew Proverb

"Of all the animosities which have existed among mankind, those which are caused by a difference of sentiments in religion appear to be the most inveterate and distressing, and ought to be deprecated." President George Washington

"America will never be destroyed from the outside. If we falter and lose our freedoms, it will be because we destroyed ourselves." Abraham Lincoln

STRETCHING YOUR MIND

Oliver Wendell Holmes, United States Supreme Court Justice, once remarked, "Man's mind, stretched to a new idea, never goes back to its original dimensions." Stretching tends to cause us to get out of our comfort zone. Most of us really like our comfort zone and are reluctant to move out of it. Some of us never seem to get out of that comfort zone. But when we do move out of that comfort zone with thought and planning consistent with our faith, we can find new rewards.

There are two ways to move out of our comfort zone. One is by our actions and the other is in our thoughts. Let's talk about actions first. Greeting a visitor at church might require moving out of our comfort zone but it not only has personal rewards, we are also following God's commands (see Matthew 28 and John 3). Other actions outside of our comfort zone might be to do something you haven't done before, going to a new place, trying a new food, accepting a new job and making new friends. With good planning and acting consistent with our faith, most of these experiences will turn out well.

But what Oliver Wendell Holmes had in mind was to stretch our mind by learning new things, exposure to new information, entertaining ideas not previously considered. In doing so we should never entertain that which would be inconsistent with our faith. Isaiah 26:3 adds this helpful advice: "You will keep in perfect peace those whose minds are steadfast, because they trust in you."

In fact, a careful reading of the Bible will stretch our mind as we encounter God at work in the lives of people and in us. The human mind is fascinating. Through reading, meeting new people and having new experiences, we can gain a fresh perspective that is deeper and more meaningful. The world around us is amazing. Stretching the mind to learn more about the world we live in and the people within it can be one of the great rewards of life. Seek out an interesting Christian person and start asking them questions about faith and life. Pick up a book on a topic where you have little knowledge. Travel to a place you have not visited before. As you encounter these new experiences, write down some of your thoughts. You will discover new aspects of who you are. Try stretching your mind by learning something new or gaining a new perspective today.

STUDY QUESTIONS

1. Write down six new experiences you have had in the past year including places you have been, people you have met, experiences you have had, books or other media you have read or seen. How have these experiences changed you?
2. Stretching your mind means getting to a point in life when you say to yourself, that's a new way of looking at things (a new perspective). Has that happened to you?
3. Write down what your understanding is of the statement by Oliver Wendell Holmes. 181

"Aim at Heaven and you will get the earth thrown in.
Aim at earth and you get neither." C. S. Lewis

"What good is it, my brother, if a man claims to have faith but has no deeds? Can such faith save him? James 2:14

RIGHT THINKING

Let's think about what Leo Tolstoy called "right thinking." We tend to believe that when people agree with us that they are thinking properly. After all, we certainly know and speak the truth. However, when we think and then speak or write, we do so within societal norms (including laws) which say there are certain kinds of behavior that will draw a penalty and others that will be applauded. Even more important is our personal value system. Greatly affected by our parents and others around us as we grow up, this value system tells us what is right and what is wrong. As adult Christians our value system is refined by the Bible which gives us absolute truths to guide us. So we have three sources that help us to find "right thinking."

Leo Tolstoy used the term "free thinkers" to describe those who would go beyond the societal norms and laws and beyond many of the values we were taught growing up to seek the truth. He described these people as "willing to use their mind without prejudice and without fearing to understand things that clash with their own customs, privileges or beliefs." Tolstoy adds, "This state of mind is not common but it is essential for right thinking; where it is absent, discussion is apt to become worse than useless."

Let's look at the statement by Leo Tolstoy. First, it is impossible for us to completely get beyond our own prejudices. A prejudice is a strongly held belief that cannot be entirely supported by logical reasoning or facts. Think about your strong opinions concerning the food you eat, behaviors of other people, things that frustrate you. Second, any time we look at the world around us, we are standing in our own value system and this provides our worldview. We see the world through the glasses of our own value system.

So is there some value in Tolstoy's comment about "right thinking?" Tolstoy was urging us to look at something new to us that doesn't fit into our current thinking and at least consider its merits rather than make a quick rebuttal. Thomas Edison went against societal norms when his thinking led him to believe that there could be an electric light bulb. His personal values told him it couldn't happen. But he was willing to consider information that others had not utilized to lead him to a great discovery. We all must respect our faith and our values but there might be new information, new insights, that could lead us to "right thinking."

STUDY QUESTIONS 150

1. Describe some thought that you have had which goes beyond societal norms and is new insight, a new perspective, on some person, place or thing.
2. How does your Christian faith relate to developing new ideas, new perspectives, and new insights?
3. "Group think" is the term psychologists apply to what happens when one person in a group speaks up with a strong conclusion and no one in the group dares to dissent, thinking that they are alone in their perspective. Have you faced this situation in a group but had the courage to speak up with a different perspective?

150

"To love God with our minds means that we think differently about the way we live and love, the way we worship and serve, the way we work to earn our livelihood, the way we learn and teach." Dr. David Dockery

"I am the vine; you are the branches. If a man remains in me and I in him, he will bear much fruit; apart from me you can do nothing." John 15:5

"A life in Christ does not remove us from the world, it sustains us in it." Pastor Dr. David Jeremiah

STANDING UP FOR WHAT IS RIGHT

To stand up for what is right requires that we must first come to understand what is right. This, in return, requires us to develop or accept some standard against which to measure various behaviors to determine what is right. The Bible is our best guide in finding standards against which behavior can be judged. The Bible contains some very specific directives about behavior but in other areas there are only general guidelines to tell us what is right. But the Bible does tell us that "in all things love." When a behavior is done in genuine love, it is likely to be right behavior, assuming others do not misguide the person about how to demonstrate love. Any behavior motivated by hatred is bound to be wrong behavior. The Apostle Paul exhorts us through I Corinthians 16:13: "Be on our guard; stand firm in the faith; be courageous; be strong."

Now let's assume that we have figured out what behavior is right and good. Let's also assume that we will try to do what is right ourselves in our encounters with others. This still leaves the big area of the behavior of others in our presence and within our knowledge. Do we have the courage to stand up for what is right? Do we have the courage to challenge others who commit unlawful, unethical or sinful behavior?

When we fail to speak up or fail to act when unlawful, unethical or sinful behavior is done in our presence or within our knowledge, we are implying that we accept that behavior. When we give the appearance of accepting bad behavior, we are actually encouraging such behavior to continue or be repeated.

When we look the other way, we are committing our own sin, our own unethical behavior. We cannot logically be critical of behavior that we are unwilling to challenge or report. Deitrich Bonhoeffer, the German pastor who spoke up against Nazi Germany, was eventually killed by the Nazis. He asked others, "Will you speak up for what is right?"

We might be tempted to think that others have the responsibility for correcting what is wrong. Or we might rationalize that if I speak up, others will criticize me or it might take my time and effort to be a witness. What if something happens to you and you need a witness but those who could be witnesses tell you it would be too bothersome for them? Don't expect others to be good citizens unless <u>you</u> are willing to do <u>your</u> part by speaking up for what is right. Are you willing to stand up for what is right?

STUDY QUESTIONS

1. Do you feel you have a good understanding of what is right in God's sight?
2. What are the likely circumstances in your work and lifestyle in which you will have the opportunity to stand up for what is right? Will you have the courage to stand up for what is right when the time comes?
3. Think of a time when someone else stood up for what was right at the time and how you felt about it or were impacted by it.

171A

"Truth is so obscure in these times, and falsehood so established, that unless we love the truth, we cannot know it." Blaise Pascal

"When a person thinks outside the normal boundaries, interesting things might happen." Anonymous

"With a half-hearted effort, don't expect great results."

DOING THE RIGHT THING

Most of us <u>want</u> to do the right thing. Typically, our first thought when wanting to do the right thing is to ponder what do we want. Wrong approach. This would be an egocentric approach. The right questions to ask, in the proper order are a) what is God's will, b) what does the situation require and c) how can I make a positive intervention? Start by looking outside of yourself, not inside.

First, what is God's will? Our greatest temptation here is to confuse our will with God's will. We think about what we want and then rationalize that this must be what God wants. Wrong approach. Seeking God's will starts with submission of self to prayer. Earnest prayer, not "God please give me what I want?" Sometimes it takes time. When we feel we have God's will, even if it makes us uncomfortable, we need to act upon God's will. Jesus affectionately expressed His honor of those who focus on God's will as he said, recorded in Mark 3:35: "Whoever does God's will is my brother and sister and mother."

Second, what does the situation require? Doing the right thing requires understanding the situation, knowing the setting, getting a feel for what is happening, perceiving what is required under the circumstances. This requires looking outside of yourself. It requires being observant of what forces are at work and the direction they are taking as well as a perception of not only the current situation but also what the situation is changing into. Observe people, what they are saying and what they are doing. What are their concerns? What would make the situation a happy one? Understand the dynamics of the situation.

Thirdly, what part of my gifts, talents, education and experience can I draw upon to make this a positive intervention? This is a matching process. Each of us has some contrasting abilities. We can be happy or we can grieve with someone else. We can urge action or urge caution. We can motivate or we can calm down a situation. The point is that to intervene positively, we must adjust ourselves to our understanding of the situation and not try to make the situation fit what we want the situation to be. Only after we do that can we help steer the situation toward a positive end point. <u>Understand and then act.</u> Don't act and try to understand later unless the building is on fire.

To follow this three step approach, we must begin by thinking outside of ourselves. Focus on God's will and the situation around us. Then, and only then, can we focus on identifying and doing the right thing.

STUDY QUESTIONS

1. Find a quiet place to pray and then earnestly open up yourself to hear what God has to say to you about the situation you are considering.
2. Seek first to understand before acting. What is the real situation, not just your first impulse?
3. What in your talents, gifts, education and experience could help make a situation a better one, help you to do the right thing? 172

"A wise man talks because he has something to say. Fools talk because they have to say something." Anonymous

"A wise man changes his mind. A fool never will." Spanish Proverb

"Interesting people say interesting things that others should consider." Anonymous

"Let us, by all wise and constitutional measures, promote intelligence among the people, as the best means of preserving our liberties." President James Monroe

"Pride only breeds quarrels, but wisdom is found in those who take advice." Proverbs 13:10

"You change your life by changing your heart." Max Lucado

CHAPTER FOUR

WISDOM AND LIVING, LEGACY

Rules of Life, Rationale For Life, John Wooden, Lou Holtz, Writing Your Obituary, Significance, Gratitude, Meeting Others Halfway, Acquiring Wisdom, Rights and Responsibilities, Being a Masterpiece, Opportunity, Accountability, Five Most Interesting People, Finding Beauty In Nature, How We Are Remembered, Acquiring Wisdom

ACCOUNTABILITY FOR WHAT WE DON'T DO

Instead of responsibility for what we do, let's talk about being accountable for what we <u>don't do</u>. The 17th century French playwright and actor Moliere made the comment, "it is not only what we do, but also what we do not do, for which we are accountable." There are more things that we do not do each day than the things we actually do. So this might be our defense when asked why we did not do something others might have wanted us to do. Obviously, there are many things not done around us for which we cannot be held accountable.

So what <u>might</u> we be held accountable for <u>not doing?</u> Accountability for inaction can be narrowed down to whether six factors exist: 1) opportunity, 2) capability, 3) compatibility with our value system (something that we think would be the right thing to do), 4) adequate time and the right time, 5) equipment (if required) and 6) location (being in the right place). The basic concept here is <u>not acting</u> when we <u>should have acted</u>. Let's look at these factors in order.

<u>First</u> is opportunity. The opportunity could have multiple steps such as making contact, completing an application, follow-up and obtaining

information. Opportunity does not necessarily mean an invitation or someone asking you to do something. It simply means that the opportunity could have been taken. Second, we must have the talent, education and skill to accomplish what we see as the right thing to do as well as understand the opportunity.

Third, compatibility with our values. Not all possible acts are the right thing to do. Our values tell us to refrain from some things and to pursue others. The basic question is: should we have acted? Fourth, is there adequate time and is the timing right? There must be a sufficient amount of time available to complete the right thing and our timing for us to have been there at the right time.

Fifth, if the task requires certain equipment or tools that such items are readily available at the right time. Sixth, being in the right place. We have to be at the right location to take appropriate action.

All of this comes down to the desire, the motivation to do the right thing. Even if all of the factors mentioned above are present, if we don't want to do the right thing because it looks like work or is inconvenient, we can be held accountable for what we failed to do when we had the opportunity to do the right thing. James 4:17 tells us, "If anyone, then, knows the good they ought to do and doesn't do it, it is sin for them." The action could be as simple as saying thank you at the right moment. When that moment is passed and the six factors above are met but we did not act, we should be held accountable for failing to act appropriately.

When we are held accountable for something we did not do but should have done, what are the options we have? Sometimes we can correct the action. In other instances, we might apologize, make amends in some other way such as doing a favor for an offended person or just resolve to avoid such a failure to act in the future. To do nothing as a result of the failure to act means we will likely make the same mistake again. As Christians we are told to love one another and this means we will act in the best interests of others. The best interests of others will lead to taking responsibility for what we didn't do.

BEING A MASTERPIECE

Thomas Crum made this statement: "What would it be like if you lived each day, each breath, as a work of art in progress? Imagine that you are a masterpiece unfolding every second of every day, a work of art taking form with every breath." What does it take to be a personal masterpiece? The Bible is a good place to start in our search. The Bible presents two avenues to become a personal masterpiece. One is to follow the precepts in the New Testament for acceptable behavior. Second is seeking the will of God for our lives. The first provides general guidelines while the second is specific to us.

Henry Drummond wrote the classic *The Greatest Thing in the World* in which he makes the case that most important thing is love based on the New Testament. He explains the concept of love as having nine components: patience, kindness, generosity, humility, courtesy, unselfishness, good temper, guilelessness and sincerity. Now if each of us would be guided by love and sought to achieve each of these nine components to the extent of our ability, how close would we come toward being a personal masterpiece in the sight of God?

But we must add another ingredient. God did not intend for each of us to be a copy of everyone else. God has a plan for each of us while we exhibit all of the characteristics of love (toward God, others and God's universe). To seek God's will, we must first become acutely aware of who we are. What are the gifts God created within us? How are we able to develop these gifts through education, experience and practice? God's will for us is always consistent with the characteristics of love described in the New Testament. We can seek His will for us through prayer, self-discovery of our gifts and talents and through continuous effort on our part.

The Apostle Paul writing to the Christians in Ephesus 2:10 said, "For we are God's handiwork, created in Christ Jesus to do good works, which God prepared in advance for us to do." The word "handiwork" in the Greek language is the word "poema" from which we get the word "poem" in the English language. Those of us who follow Christ are God's poetry, yes, His masterful handiwork through the regenerating work of Christ and the Holy Spirit. It is up to us to combine the characteristics of love with

God's will for us and then our effort to develop ourselves in keeping with that will of God. Do the nine characteristics of love describe you? Are you seeking God's will? Are you in prayer? Are you a "masterpiece unfolding every second of every day"?

STUDY QUESTIONS

1. Consider developing a list of the nine characteristics of love as described by Drummond and then write down a personal assessment of how well you think you are doing with each of them.

2. Give some serious thought and prayer to what God's will is for your life. Make notes on all of the elements that you think are part of God's will for you.

3. What are you doing to combine love and God's will for you? Prayer, thought, planning, education, experience and practice are all places to start. 137

"My dear brothers, take note of this: Everyone should be quick to listen, slow to speak and slow to become angry, for man's anger does not bring about the righteous life that God desires." James 1:19

MY THIRTEEN RULES

My Thirteen Rules comes from the book, *It Worked For Me*, by General Colin Powell. Gen. Powell served as Chairman of the Joint Chiefs of Staff, the highest military position in the United States and as Secretary of State with President George W Bush. General Powell developed thirteen rules from "quotes and aphorisms" that he had collected and some he had "made up over the years." They originally appeared in Parade magazine. Here they are with a comment or two to explain them further.

1. "IT AIN'T AS BAD AS YOU THINK. IT WILL LOOK BETTER IN THE MORNING." "This rule reflects an attitude, not a prediction."
2. "GET MAD AND THEN GET OVER IT." Everyone gets mad but "my experience is that staying mad is not useful."
3. "AVOID HAVING YOUR EGO SO CLOSE TO YOUR POSITION THAT WHEN YOUR POSITION FALLS, YOUR EGO GOES WITH IT." Don't let your argument for something be so closely tied to your ego that when you lose the argument or have to compromise that your ego goes with it.
4. "IT CAN BE DONE." It's more about attitude than reality.
5. "BE CAREFUL ABOUT WHAT YOU CHOOSE, YOU MIGHT GET IT." Don't rush into things.
6. "DON'T LET ADVERSE FACTS STAND IN THE WAY OF A GOOD DECISION." In a tough decision, use information and instinct.
7. "YOU CAN'T MAKE SOMEONE ELSE'S CHOICES. YOU SHOULDN'T LET SOMEONE ELSE MAKE YOURS." Take responsibility for what you do and fail to do.
8. "CHECK SMALL THINGS." "Success ultimately rests on small things, lots of small things."
9. "SHARE CREDIT." "Share the credit down and around the whole organization."
10. "REMAIN CALM, BE KIND." "Establish a calm zone but retain a sense of urgency." "Have a healthy zone of emotions."
11. "HAVE A VISION, BE DEMANDING." "Followers need to know where their leaders are taking them and for what purpose."

12. "DON'T TAKE COUNSEL OF YOUR FEARS OR NAYSAYERS." "Fear is normal and has to be overcome. Naysayers are everywhere."

13. "PERPETUAL OPTIMISM IS A FORCE MULTIPLIER." "Perpetual optimism, believing in yourself, believing in your purpose, believing you will prevail, and demonstrating passion and confidence is a force multiplier."

These are the thirteen rules of General Colin Powell, Four Star General in the United States Army and U S Secretary of State. Proverbs 18:15 summarizes what he had to say: "The heart of the discerning acquires knowledge, for the ears of the wise seek it out." Which of the thirteen rules could apply to you today?

STUDY QUESTIONS

1. Which of the Thirteen Rules has the most relevance for your life today? Why is that?

2. Much of what General Powell wrote is about attitude. Describe your attitude today. Is it positive enough to implement these Thirteen Rules?

3. What does General Powell mean by a "force multiplier?" How could you apply this concept to your life?

332

STATUE OF LOU HOLTZ

On the campus of Notre Dame University in South Bend, Indiana, there stands a statue of Lou Holtz. For those of you who are not football fans, Lou Holtz was at one time the football coach at Notre Dame. He also coached at Minnesota, South Carolina and Arkansas. Now retired, he is a popular speaker on campuses and in corporate settings. Lou Holtz likes to tell others about the rules he followed that made him a formidable success on the gridiron. Lou tells us that each of us should have a vision and a plan. The vision is of what we want to make happen. The plan is how we are going to accomplish it. Basic to his philosophy is that in our plans we have three rules we should follow. Here is what he said:

1. DO WHAT IS RIGHT. There is never a right time to do the wrong thing. You are the person in control of your attitude. Never let another person control your attitude. When things aren't going well, you need to be a leader with a positive attitude. Having the right attitude is more important than having talent. Don't dwell on mistakes. It is wrong to be bitter; this is always negative. If in doubt about what is right, look at the Bible. Your conscience can be your guide about what is right and your conscience can guide you in a wide variety of situations. Doing what is right could take courage. If so, muster up the courage to do the right thing. It could take courage as well to do the wrong thing. But the results are so different.

2. DO WHAT YOU DO TO THE BEST OF YOUR ABILITY. Lou Holtz said he was born with a golden spoon because he was taught by his parents. Parents need to encourage their children to work at the best of their ability whatever that ability level might be. We should all be committed to excellence. We should not be concerned about being popular because wanting to be popular will lead us away from doing our best. Focus on what you are doing.

3. SHOW PEOPLE YOU CARE. When you receive recognition, pass it on to others. When you are part of a team, you can't do it alone. You can't be a success without sacrifice. Caring can make a big difference in the life of another person and it will help you as well. Being significant is when you help others to be successful.

The above is a paraphrase of statements by Lou Holtz. Coach Holtz also added this thought. He said there are four things all of us need to have in our lives: We need to have something to do, someone to love, something to believe in and something to hope for. He made it clear that he believes in Jesus Christ. In speaking at a college commencement, he told the audience, "I've been 21 but you've never been 78." He was encouraging them to listen to what he had to say. Every one of us can benefit from applying what Coach Lou Holtz had to say. Which of his thoughts have the most relevance for you? Think about how and why they have this relevance. Also consider Proverbs 21:5: "The plans of the diligent lead to profit as surely as haste leads to poverty." Then take some action.

STUDY QUESTIONS

1. Of the three major points by Coach Lou Holtz, which one strikes you as the one with the most application to you? Why is that? What are you doing about it?
2. Lou Holtz made the statement that all of us need something to do. Do you agree? What are you doing?
3. Describe three things you have done in the past 24 hours that demonstrates that you care about others.

329

JOHN WOODEN'S SEVEN PRINCIPLES

John Wooden had Seven Principles. If you don't follow sports, basketball in particular, you might not know who John Wooden was. Coach Wooden was best known as the basketball coach at UCLA where his teams won ten NCAA championships including seven in a row. His teams won 88 consecutive games over four seasons. He was a charter member of the NABC National Basketball Hall of Fame.

So why are we talking about basketball and Coach Wooden? When Coach finished the 8th grade, his father gave him a handwritten card and told him, "Son, try to live up to this." They became John Wooden's seven principles. Let's talk about those seven principles that guided this very successful coach throughout his 99-year life ending in 2010.

As a Christian, Coach Wooden based his seven principles on Matthew 22:37-39 where we are told to first, love the Lord your God and then to love your neighbor. His first principle was, "Be true to yourself." Coach Wooden added, "You must know who you are and be true to who you are if you are going to be who you can and should become." "You must have the courage to be true to yourself." It is tempting to yield to pressures in life and become the person others would have you be. We need to know our values and stick to them.

The second principle was "Help others." Coach was known for his many so-called "Woodenisms." On this topic he added, "You have not lived a perfect day until you've done something for somebody who cannot repay you."

The third principle was "Make each day your masterpiece." Coach added, "Make every moment count. Be productive. Build balance in your life. Keep your priorities in order." One way to be productive is the fourth principle, "Drink deeply from Good Books, Especially the Bible." Coach added, "Poetry, biographies, and all the other great books will greatly enrich your life." "God's greatest gift for our time on earth is His Word." Coach read his Bible regularly.

The fifth principle was "Make Friendship a Fine Art." Coach commented, "It's friendship when you do good things for each other." Sixth, "Build a Shelter against a Rainy Day by the Life You Live." Coach's father didn't mean to just have a money shelter; he meant to live your life so that humility is one of your qualities. The seventh principle was "Pray for guidance and counsel, and give thanks for your blessings every day." Prayer is how we reach God to give thanks and seek guidance and counsel. God blesses each of us. When you pray, ask God to help <u>you</u> to make Coach Wooden's seven principles work. How well would these seven principles work in your life?

STUDY QUESTIONS

1. Which of the seven principles is the most meaningful in your life?
2. Is there one of the principles that you find difficult to carry out? Which one is it and why is it difficult? What are you going to do about it?
3. If you could add an 8th principle, what would it be?

239

Note: Quotes are from Pat Williams, *Coach Wooden, The 7 Principles That Shaped His Life and Will Change Yours* (Revell, 2011)

RIGHTS AND RESPONSIBILITIES

When was the last time you saw people demonstrating for their responsibilities? I never have. We often see people demonstrating for their rights however.

A basic principle is that rights and responsibilities must be roughly equal. With any new right will come responsibilities, even though we tend to like our rights more than our responsibilities. This also means when we take on new responsibilities, new rights should come with it.

It is surely an important value for each Christian to meet each of their responsibilities. In fact, the Apostle Paul said so much in his exhortation to the Christians in Galatia. In Galatians 6:5 Paul said: "...for each one should carry their own load."

As a person moves into adulthood, new rights are given such as the right to vote, the right to own real estate and cars and to be treated as other adults. But in the exercise of those rights, we must act responsibly. What does it mean to act responsibly? It means we must not abuse our right by using it carelessly or in disregard for the law and the rights of others. It means that we need to make contributions back to society instead of just claiming certain rights from society. Making contributions means helping to make this a better world by the things that we think, say and do. Hopefully, our contributions will outweigh our exercise of rights so that we can improve society instead of just benefitting from it.

Think about your rights and responsibilities. Are you enjoying your rights? What responsibilities do you have? Are the two roughly equal? What are you doing to exercise your rights and meet your responsibilities?

STUDY QUESTIONS

1. To what extent is where you live the reason that you have both rights and responsibilities?

2. What contributions do you make to society that go beyond your rights and responsibilities?
3. For the system to work, we must exercise our rights. Have you voted in every election in recent years?

58

"But the things that proceed out of the mouth come from the heart, and those defile the man. 'For out of the heart come evil thoughts, murders, adulteries, fornications, thefts, false witness, slanders'" Matthew 15:18-19

"So then each one of us will give an account of himself to God" Romans 14:21

RESPONSIBILITY

How will you act responsibly in the next year? I Corinthians 7:24 reads: "Brothers, and sisters, each person, as responsible to God, should remain in the situation they were in when God called them." The context here is pointing out to slave and free men, that whatever their role in life, they are responsible to God and any other allegiance second. When a person is responsible to God and then others, it means there is an allegiance, a desire to please, and a desire to do what is required. Applying this teaching to today, it means that all of us are responsible to God first. In 1 Peter 1:18 we hear that man "was redeemed from the empty way of life…" "with the precious blood of Christ." Then there are responsibilities to others.

What are we responsible for doing or being? The New Testament gives many lessons on what kind of persons we are to be and how we are to behave (I Peter has many examples). These lessons cover the many facets of life including our relationships with one another and our relationship to God. The Bible has ample references to being responsible so that there is no excuse for us today to say that we know not what to do.

Even with those many lessons, we still struggle in applying these truths to our everyday actions with each other. Each of us has a responsibility to others, whether Christian or not. Each of us has a struggle between God and self as we attempt to live the lives God wants us to live. However, the closer we are in communion with God, the smaller the gap between what we think that we want and our understanding of what God wants for us. Mother Teresa and many other Christian examples have closed most of that gap by endeavoring to live God's way without the trappings of our society. However, we are born as sinners and must continually work at how we can close the gap between our desires and the mandates of God.

Accepting responsibility means accepting the results of our actions. Negative outcomes from our actions are not to be blamed on others or on God. When we have done something less than perfect (and we do every day), God expects us to act responsibly by correcting or compensating for our shortcomings. Being responsible means not only making amends for our wrong doings but also taking responsibility for becoming the person

God would like for us to become. We must ask for forgiveness. This means we must take the initiative and not just sit back and try to avoid making mistakes. Taking the initiative means setting goals and working out how to make those goals achievable. Further, it means we are expected to do this all of the years that God has given us on earth. Each of us has been given spiritual gifts that we need to develop and utilize in Christian service to others and self.

If we seek to be close to God, we will want to accept the responsibility of being one of His followers. That requires a daily effort in reading the Bible, prayer, maintaining a Christian life as directed by the Bible and serving others according to the opportunities given to us and asking for forgiveness when we sin. Are you ready to accept this responsibility?

STUDY QUESTIONS

1. What does being responsible to God mean to you?
2. What daily efforts are you engaged in that supports your allegiance to God?
3. In what ways are you being responsible for the lives of others?

318

"It is not so much that we are too bold to endure rules; it is rather that we are too timid to endure responsibilities." G. K. Chesterton

FIVE MOST IMPORTANT PEOPLE

Other programs have been about favorite people or people we admire while in this program we will look at the five most <u>important</u> people in your life to date. These are not necessarily people you are fond of or the people you love the most. What distinguishes these people from others is the influence they have had on your life to date. These are people who have shaped your life. They could be a spouse, parents, teachers, pastors, neighbors, friends, co-workers, an uncle or aunt or someone you met in some other way. The most important person to have an impact in our lives is the Lord himself. Isaiah in 40:31 said, "...but those who hope in the Lord will renew their strength. They will soar on wings like eagles; they will run and not grow weary, they will walk and not be faint."

This influence could have come from decisions they made, decisions they helped you to make or situations in which you drew from the experience or wisdom of the individual with or without their knowledge. If you have allowed a negative experience to shape your life, one of the five most important people in your life could have been a negative experience. If you are really in charge of your own life, however, as all adults should be, then you will have overcome a negative experience and possibly built something positive out of it.

Each person has certain pivotal points in life. It might be when you decided to follow Jesus. It might be a decision to go to college or not to go to college but join the armed services instead. It might be a decision to marry, a career decision, a location decision or a decision to do something unique. In any case, there were probably people who had a major influence on you at those important decision points in your life.

While a student in a community college, I had a history professor who caused me to have a lifelong interest in history influencing me to major in history, teach history in a high school and obtain graduate degrees in the field. Are there people in your life who had a similar impact on you?

Where and how we spend our time will determine which people are likely to have an influence on us. Thus it is important to spend time in positive places rather than with people who will have a negative impact on our lives. Time in church beats time in a bar.

Now think about those five people who had the greatest impact on your life. Make a list over a period of a day or two. Review it with a close friend to see what they might say. You might want to say thank you to each of these people if they are still living for the positive experiences they have provided for you.

STUDY QUESTIONS

1. Who are the five people who had the greatest impact on your life? In what way was their impact?
2. Think of five pivotal points in your life when your life started off in a different direction.
3. Who are the five people you think <u>you</u> might be impacting in a major way? 79

"But thanks be to God, who giveth us the victory through our Lord Jesus Christ" 1 Corinthians 15:57 KJV

"Nothing brings greater happiness than to serve a cause greater than self." Senator John McCain

MEETING PEOPLE HALFWAY

Henry Boye is quoted as saying; "The most important trip you might take in life is meeting people halfway." Meeting people halfway implies compromise. How do you feel about compromise?

A bully (adolescent or adult) tries to avoid any compromise intending instead to roll over others regardless of the ethics or appropriateness of the situation. A wise person knows the difference between principles and preferences, between what is really important and what is less important. Compromise means negotiation. A successful negotiation ends up being a win-win situation. Negotiation requires knowing what is really important to each party and finding the means by which as little of what is good for one party detracts from what is good for the other party(ies). A win/lose situation tends to be a situation that will soon come unglued with unpleasant activities associated.

So meeting people halfway means knowing what is really important to you, what your principles as well as your goals are. Once this is determined, it is possible to look at the rest and see what is negotiable in order to gain what is essential. It can be of considerable advantage in any negotiation to also know what is essential (principles) and what is preference (desired but not essential) for any other party to the negotiation. By knowing this, it paves the way toward exchanging issues so that both parties gain what is most essential.

What does it mean to meet people halfway? It means recognizing the issues on which you are willing to compromise, your preferences as opposed to your principles. This means you have to be able to tell the difference between a principle and a preference. Second, identify as much as possible what the other's principles and preferences are and, as clearly as possible, distinguish the difference. Third, identify the preferences you have that would have the most meaning for those with whom you are compromising. The ideal is that one of your preferences is a principle for the others. By identifying preferences on both sides, the area of negotiation becomes clear. Once others see that they are being met halfway, they are more likely to come halfway themselves. Once this happens, compromise is possible.

God wants us to live in peace and love. In order to have peace and love, we must seek ways to accept others and to find common ground with them. What can you do to meet others halfway?

STUDY QUESTIONS

1. Do you know the difference between your principles and your preferences?
2. Are there issues in your life on which you need to meet others halfway?
3. Look at the Scriptures for passages that tell us to seek peace and love with all of mankind. Which passage is the most meaningful to you?

203

"This is how we know what love is: Jesus Christ laid down His life for us. And we ought to lay down our lives for our brothers." Apostle John 1 John 3:16

"For we wrestle not against flesh and blood, but against principalities, against powers, against the rulers of the darkness of this world, against spiritual wickedness in high places. Wherefore, take unto you the whole armor of God, that you may be able to withstand in the evil day, and having done all, to stand" Ephesians 6:12-13 KJV

WHO OR WHAT HAVE YOU INVESTED IN?

When we think of investments we tend to think of money being placed in some organization where they will use the money and give us interest in return for the use of our money. All of us should make monetary investments if possible so that our financial security in the future can be more secure.

There is another kind of investment that has even greater rewards but we might not ever see the reward. This is when we invest in people. How do we do this? Some of the ways are encouragement, enablement, service, teaching and just being available to stand or sit with someone in need.

Encouragement can be a small thing like a compliment to a person for a job well done or it could mean a number of conversations extended over a period of time in which help is given to a person at work through a stressful issue. Encouragement is providing another person with support for what they are doing or have done. It means believing in them.

Enablement is when we make it possible for something to happen for someone when it would have been difficult if not impossible for him or her to do alone.

Service is when we act on behalf of someone to their benefit. It can range from opening a door for someone to providing a daily service over years.

Teaching is helping a person to learn skills and information helpful to them in life. When we teach a child or an adult, we are making an investment in that person's life. Remember the exhortation of Proverbs 3:27: "Do not withhold good from those to whom it is due, when it is in your power to act." What personal investments have <u>you</u> made this week?

STUDY QUESTIONS

1. Are you making regular investments? Identify two from the last year.
2. Has someone made an investment in you? What did they do?
3. What would you have to do in order to be an enabler?

75

"The time to guard against corruption and tyranny is before they shall have gotten hold of us. It is better to keep the wolf out of the fold than to trust to drawing his teeth and talons after he shall have entered." President Thomas Jefferson

"With malice toward none; with charity to all; with firmness in the right, as God gives us to see the right, let us strive on to finish the work we are in; to bind up the nation's wounds." President Abraham Lincoln

"I am the good shepherd. The good shepherd gives His life for His sheep." Jesus Christ in John 10:11

PEOPLE WE ADMIRE

What we admire tells a lot about our own values. We admire what we think is important. What is important to you as you look at the people around you? The Bible suggests a starting place in Philippians 4:8: "Finally, brothers and sisters, whatever is true, whatever is noble, whatever is right, whatever is pure, whatever is lovely, whatever is admirable – if anything is excellent or praiseworthy – think about such things."

Some of the things we admire in others are characteristics we wish that we could personally possess (maybe already do to some extent). They could include such characteristics as courage, knowledge, wisdom, charm, personality, faith, commitment, intelligence and wit. We see some of these characteristics in some people but rarely all of them in one person. Nonetheless, we hold these characteristics high in our value system and we wish that we had more of these characteristics than we think that we have. We have been working on attaining these characteristics with varying success and we might excel in one or more of them.

There are some characteristics that we want others to have that we don't particularly want for ourselves. We admire characteristics in the opposite gender that are not features we would want. We might look at various occupational roles and be glad that someone else wants that role when we do not want it. Nonetheless, they are characteristics we consider important.

There are some characteristics that we frown upon when we see them in others. The Pharisees apparently did this often 2,000 years ago thinking that this was evidence that they were better than others. Do you sometimes pat yourself on the back for being better than some people you see?

The characteristic of possessing a strong Christian faith should be the most basic of what we admire. When we have faith and follow what Jesus told us, many of the most desirable characteristics will appear. Of the characteristics we wish we could personally possess to a greater degree, are you actively involved in achieving them to the extent that you would want? What sacrifices would you need to make to achieve this? Any ethical compromises? What about God's plan for the person He wants you to become?

STUDY QUESTIONS

1. How close do you compare to the people you admire the most? What are the significant differences?
2. What are you doing about these significant differences?
3. Is there a person you could help in developing into the person God would have that person become?

70

"Somewhere out in the audience (might) even be someone who will one day follow in my footsteps, and preside over the White House as the President's spouse. I wish him well." Barbara Bush

GRATITUDE

Maybe it isn't Christmas when you are reading this, so what do you have gratitude for? Is it for presents that you received at Christmas or on your birthday or maybe just that your house is quiet once again? Or is it for the people with whom you are in contact at church, work, in stores and at home? Maybe for some people who are far away who you won't see during the next Christmas season?

We tend to have gratitude for that which is most important to us. So what is important to you? Is it things or is it people, or maybe both? Gratitude is a form of saying thank you for what we have received. Ephesians 5:19-20 tells us: "...Sing and make music from your heart to the Lord, always giving thinks to God the Father for everything in the name of our Lord Jesus Christ."

We should all be thankful for the birth of Jesus Christ who then died on the cross to offer us salvation so that when this life is over, we might spend eternity with Him. This is the best gift of all and it is free if we are willing to believe and then follow a Christian life. Our gratitude for Jesus should tower over all things for which we have gratitude.

Gratitude is an attitude. It acknowledges that we are not self-sufficient. It recognizes that others do things, say things, make things and simply represent what is good in life. All of this enriches our lives and makes it possible for us to do more for others. Giving or receiving a gift implies that both parties care about the other.

When we do or say things for others, should we expect gratitude? Receiving gratitude should never be our reason for serving others – our motive should be that we want to make life more satisfying, more Christ-like, for others. Giving gratitude is more about our agape relationship with another person than it is about the gift. Where is your gratitude directed at Christmas, your birthday and the rest of the year?

STUDY QUESTIONS

1. Why do you give Christmas gifts?
2. Why do you enjoy receiving gifts whenever they come?
3. Do you have gratitude toward Jesus for His gift to you? 76

"And whoever wants to be first must be slave of all. For even the Son of Man did not come to be served, but to serve, and to give His life as a ransom for many" Mark 10:44-45

"Each of you should use whatever gift you have received to serve others, as faithful stewards of God's grace in its various forms" 1 Peter 4:10

"No servant can serve two masters. Either he will hate the one and love the other, or he will be devoted to the one and despise the other. You cannot serve God and money" Luke 16:13

A BIT MORE BEAUTIFUL

Let's think about beautiful places. One of the most beautiful places in the United States is the Bok Tower Gardens at Lake Wales, Florida. The inspiration for the gardens and the builder of it was Edward W. Bok who came to the United States from the Netherlands at age six. He became a very successful publisher and a Pulitzer Price-winning author who devoted much of his effort to humanitarian, world peace and environmental causes. In 1921 he developed the idea of building a bird sanctuary on Florida's highest point of land near to where he was spending the winter at Lake Wales, Florida. A magnificent marble tower and gardens was completed before the end of the decade with a dedication ceremony attended by President Calvin Coolidge. The tower and gardens continue to bring thousands of visitors each year to hear concerts on the world known carillon and to see the beautiful grounds.

Edward Bok said part of the inspiration came from his grandmother who told him to "Make the world a bit better or more beautiful because you have lived in it." Note that she said "more" because we are to build upon God's wonderful creation. Edward Bok not only succeeded for his generation but also for generations to come. The resident carillonneur today provides daily concerts while people stroll the beautiful gardens and see the birds.

Think about whether you have made this world "a bit better or more beautiful" as a result of your living in it. It is easy to detract from the beauty of God's creation through leaving litter of paper and cigarettes. It is not so easy to enhance the beauty of the world through our presence. This takes a conscious effort.

A friend of God's Plan for Service, Dr. Richard Baxter of Nashville, TN, plants hundreds of flowers every year and enhances the world of others by bringing flowers to them. He has made the world "a bit more beautiful." Beautiful houses, trees, lawns and various architectural creations enhance the beauty of the world. Paintings and photography capture some of this beauty. Music adds to beauty. There are many opportunities for each of us in other aspects of nature, through creating beautiful objects and through presenting ourselves in a manner that is consistent with God's radiance within us. According to the Apostle Paul in Ephesians 2:10, even we are a part of God's handiwork: "For we are God's handiwork, created in Christ Jesus to do good works, which God prepared in advance for us to do."

It is important to "make the world a bit more beautiful" in every way we can. God gave us so much to work with. But beyond this, we need to stop and enjoy the beauty. Stop sometime today to look around you at the beauty that is already here and enjoy it. While appreciating it, think of ways in which you can enhance this beauty for the enjoyment of others.

STUDY QUESTIONS

1. Describe something you have done that has made the world "a bit more beautiful.
2. What is the most beautiful place you have visited? What makes it so beautiful?
3. Is there a project of beauty on your "bucket list" of things you want to do or see in your lifetime?

147

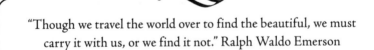

"Though we travel the world over to find the beautiful, we must carry it with us, or we find it not." Ralph Waldo Emerson

TEN DEFINING MOMENTS

Each of us has had moments when what happened helped to define who we would be for the rest of our lives. So today our topic is TEN DEFINING MOMENTS. Dr. Phil on a TV program once mentioned our topic suggesting to people that they might want to give thought to this. The suggestion prompted me to complete my list of ten defining moments. The first one I listed was being born to the parents I had. I was born into a loving, Christian home where values were taught and exemplified. A research study once reported that our values are well established by the time we are twelve or thirteen years old, including our faith.

You might have difficulty at first in coming up with ten or maybe having far more than ten. Give it more thought and some time. Come back to the list in order to get it at ten. If we list fifty we haven't narrowed it down to the most crucial moments in life. If we come up with only one or two, we need to give more thought to who we are today and what made us that way. It is suggested that you list the events in chronological order to see how one event has an effect on others later. Number seven on my list is earning a Ph.D. but that would not have happened without numbers 1-6 taking place earlier.

Now while you are involved in introspection, here is another challenge. List the seven most critical choices you have made in life. The first might be your choice of values early in life. Each of us makes hundreds of decisions every day but only a few are substantial. And among the substantial choices, only a very few (three to seven maybe) are the most critical.

The third challenge is to think of the five most pivotal people who have influenced my life (from birth). Some of them might not be alive today but they influenced us at a critical time in our life. Think about the big decisions you have made. Who influenced you to make those decisions? Who even influenced you to pose the situation in which there was a decision to be made? Let's assume that God is our most important influence in addition to these people.

Fourth, who are the five most critical people in your life today? The people you lean on for support, for making decisions, who influence you the most and the ones you love the most? This is God plus five humans impacting you now.

You will likely find that these four lists are very interesting. You have been forced to think about the most critical points in your life and the people who helped you through them. Consider the role God has played on all of these lists. You can thank the people who are still living and thank God for guiding you to be the person you are today.

STUDY QUESTIONS

1. What is the first of your ten defining moments of your life?
2. Of your seven most critical choices, are there one or two that stand out? Why is that?
3. In challenges 3 and 4 above concerning people, How many of those people were or are aware that they have been or are now critical in your life?

400

"Then Jesus directed them to have all the people sit down in groups on the green grass. So they sat down in groups of hundreds and fifties. Taking the five loaves and the two fish and looking up to heaven, He gave thanks and broke the loaves. Then He gave them to His disciples to set before the people. He also divided the fish among them all. They all ate and were satisfied, and the disciples picked up twelve baskets of broken pieces of bread and fish. The number of men who had eaten was five thousand" Mark 6:39-44

TEN SIGNIFICANT THOUGHTS

Each of these significant thoughts stands by itself and is worthy of some deep thought by each of us.

1. Jesus said, "I am the way and the truth and the life. No one comes to the Father except through me. If you really know me, you will know my Father as well." (John 14:6-7)
2. Each of us has at least one gift from God (1 Peter 4:10)
3. We are born with a sinful nature (Romans 7:17-19). Yet we are given the choice to ask for forgiveness from our sin (Acts 2:38). When we do, we can be blessed in what we do (James 1:25).
4. Until we die or our mind becomes incompetent, we are responsible for what we do and say and the impact we have on others.
5. Gratitude always works in the long run. (Col 3:16) When we have the spirit of gratitude for what has been done for us we maintain a positive view of life. This positive view helps us to see even more ways in which we should show gratitude. Our greatest gratitude should be to God for His Son's sacrifice on the cross.
6. Each crisis in life has a chance of becoming an opportunity. After a crisis we should review the situation to determine what good might come from it. In doing so, we must look beyond ourselves. How have others been impacted? Is there an opportunity for us to help?
7. "Relationships affect our physical and mental functioning throughout life. This invisible power, the power of the other, builds both the hardware and the software that leads to healthy functioning and better performance." Dr. Henry Cloud, *The Power of the Other*
8. Understanding the right thing, what we think God wants us to do, and then doing something else is disobedience and a sin (Romans 6:16).
9. Not all bad choices are a sin, some choices are just stupid. We make stupid decisions when we are distracted, when we act without thinking, when we act without consulting God in prayer.
10. While each of us needs to assume responsibility for taking care of ourselves, this is normally not a full-time job. This leaves time for us to center on the needs and hopes of others. (Mt 5:16, 7:12)

STUDY QUESTIONS

1. Which of the ten significant thoughts touched you the most? Why was that?
2. Look at #4 and #10 above. Do you accept responsibility for your life or do you feel that others are to blame for what does not go right in your life?
3. See #5 above. Are you in a spirit of gratitude for everything that has been and is being done for you including God's blessings?

305

"We are lovers of the beautiful, yet simple in taste; and we cultivate the mind without loss of manliness." Pericles (c. 495-429 B C)

"All things were made by Him; and without Him was not anything made that was made" John 1:3 KJV

OPPORTUNITIES IN EVERY DIFFICULTY

Even when difficulties press upon us or we fear that they might, we should look for the opportunities hidden in that difficulty. Or some might call it Difficulties in Every Opportunity. Why is it that some of us tend to see our difficulties more clearly than our opportunities or fail to see any opportunities when resolving a difficulty?

Opportunities come to all of us. Some are great opportunities but most of them are small ones that, used appropriately, can lead to more opportunities. The question is not whether opportunities will come our way. When they do, we must decide what action we will take with the opportunities presented to us or what opportunities we will create with some diligence on our part. Some opportunities in life are not seen because we are not looking or thinking. Other opportunities we pass up for lack of energy, self-confidence or courage (and maybe all three). Why is it that two people born on the same day, in the same part of the world, of the same gender and with the same gifts, that one person reaches his or her life goals and the other is disgruntled because the world was against him or her? Our attitude, courage and/or self-confidence can make the difference.

Some opportunities are placed in our laps while others we have to seek or earn. Each of us has at least one God-given gift. Opportunities come when we develop our gifts and take the initiative to find the opportunities inherent with that gift. When we wait for the train to come while we aren't even sitting at the station, we might not even hear the train.

When we face difficulties in life, as all of us do, some of us see the opportunity in that difficulty. It could be in how we overcome the difficulty that gives us new perspective and new hope for the future. It could be in the people we meet as we seek to overcome our difficulty. God presents us with some challenges in life for us to overcome but most of our difficulties we create. We become stronger when we persevere in overcoming difficulties and challenges. People who reach their life goals have already overcome many difficulties. Some difficulties can even be enjoyable to overcome. A person who wants to be a major league baseball player can enjoy the process of preparation and experiences. For some of us, the difficulty is that we have no life goals. We might expect that happiness will be presented to us. While that might occur for a few, a lack of effort is not likely to bring about a life situation in which we are happy.

In the process of seeking good opportunities, consider the wisdom of Solomon as recorded in Proverbs 2:6: "For the Lord gives wisdom, from His mouth come knowledge and understanding."

So what are the difficulties <u>you</u> are facing in life or think you might face in the future? Are you willing to face them head on? Are you willing to look for the opportunities in your difficulties?

STUDY QUESTIONS

1. Write down a difficulty you are facing. Describe it as fully as you can. What is your plan for overcoming this difficulty?
2. Is there an opportunity you see in this difficulty? Be aware that the opportunity might present itself as you work to overcome the difficulty (challenge).
3. Are you the person who tends to focus on the difficulties in every opportunity rather than taking advantage of the opportunity? What could you do about this?

340

"Once you realize there is a life after mistakes, you get a self-confidence that never goes away." Bob Schieffer

SIGNIFICANCE

What is real significance? In our society we tend to think of significance as the position we hold, how many fans we have, winning the Nobel Prize or an award for best actor or the best player in the sport. This significance shows up in a person's name being in the history books as President of the United States or recipient of the Dove Award. Being a General in time of war or starring in the film having the most gate receipts is what the public gives acclaim to during a person's life time.

After a life is over, the acclaim dies down until it reaches insignificance. How many Roman Senators can you name? Maybe you can name those who played in the first Super Bowl? Who was Secretary of State in the Truman administration? Which team was the best in the NBA last year?

So if being famous today and hard to remember later is what happens, what is true significance? Maybe the question should be, <u>who or what</u> determines significance? Where is there a perpetual memory of everything that happens? How would even our thoughts be known and then subject to recall? As George Burns once said, "Think God."

God is omnipresent, all-knowing, the creator of the universe. God knows what we have done, what we have not done, what we have thought, what we have said, what our feelings are and have been. God knows everything about us. God knows everything about everyone. Even the heroes of today are known by God in every detail. This is all borne out by the statement Jesus made as recorded in Matthew 10:29-31: "Are not two sparrows sold for a penny? Yet not one of them will fall to the ground outside of your Father's care. And even the hairs of your head are all numbered. So don't be afraid; you are worth more than many sparrows."

The Bible has many admonitions about God's expectations of us. We are told to be obedient to God's will. Herein lies the clue to significance. Everlasting significance comes from The One who knows all about us. The real criteria for significance are found in the Bible. None of us is sinless but everyone can achieve significance in the eyes of God. To achieve significance, think of what God would consider significant for each of us.

It lies in the gifts and talents given to us and in the opportunities given to us during our lifetime. What are you doing with your gifts, talents and opportunities to achieve significance in God's eyes? How close are you to achieving the significance God intended for you?

STUDY QUESTIONS

1. What is the significance God intends for you?
2. How well are you doing on achieving this significance?
3. What do you need to do tomorrow to come closer to achieving God's significance?

216A

"For God so loved the world that He gave his one and only Son, that whoever believes in Him shall not perish but have eternal life" John 3:16

"Peter replied, 'Repent and be baptized, every one of you, in the name of Jesus Christ for the forgiveness of your sins. And you will receive the gift of the Holy Spirit. The promise is for you and your children and for all who are far off – to all whom the Lord our God will call'" Acts 2:38

IT'S NOT WHAT YOU GATHER

What is the difference between what possessions we have and what positive influence we have. An anonymous source gave us this bit of wisdom: "IT'S NOT WHAT YOU GATHER, but what you scatter that tells the kind of life that you have lived." We are likely to consider what we own as our legacy to the next generations but this is only a part of the story. We can have considerable impact upon future generations in what we pass on to them to bring them to a Christian faith, make their lives easier and to make more things possible in their lives. This can be a Christian life with money, physical possessions, reputation, principles on how to live our lives and a great example. We should endeavor in this life to prepare our children and their children for eternal life as well as society for the years to come.

If we are guided by another anonymous quote: "He who has the most toys at the end wins," then we will want to gather the most real estate and physical objects by the time we die to consider that we have won. Won what? If having the most toys is the object of our life, we have missed the reason of why God created us. The toys can be the diversion Satan puts before us to attract us down his path. The people who are the most admired are not the wealthiest or those who appear to have the most toys. We all desire to have some of the toys of life and the Bible does not condemn having the toys of life. The Bible condemns making them #1 in our life. Look at the life of Job. Job had much but it was taken from him to see if he would turn away from God. Job stayed firm in his faith (Job 13:15: "Though He slay me, yet will I hope in Him"). Note that Job ended life with many possessions.

The quote at the beginning of this message suggests that there is something more important than the things we gather. Let's repeat it: "It's not what you gather, but what you scatter that tells the kind of life that you have lived." What is it that we "scatter?" We are told in the Scripture to have a strong faith and to love one another so as to be servants of others. We influence and serve others every day. We "scatter" by our relationship to God, our faith and principles of life that we share, what we say, what we do, the influence we have, how we utilize our time, how we utilize our gifts and resources, how we relate to other people and how we take care of ourselves. Note that power and the number of toys we have are not on the list. What we "scatter" today and tomorrow will build the legacy that will tell "the kind of life that you have lived." What will others say about what and how you scattered during your lifetime?

STUDY QUESTIONS

1. How are you doing on the scale between gathering and scattering?
2. Scattering should relate to your talents and gifts as well as your education and experience. What does that suggest in terms of where you should "scatter?"
3. Is there an area of life in which you feel you could have some positive influence on the lives of others but you haven't yet gotten around to get involved? What is that area? When and how are you going to get involved?
4. Are there principles of life by which you live that you could share with others to help live the kind of life that would please God?

241A

"And to godliness brotherly kindness; and to brotherly kindness, charity" II Peter 1:7

"Therefore, as God's chosen people, holy and dearly loved, clothe yourselves with compassion, kindness, humility, gentleness and patience. Bear with each other and forgive one another if any of you has a grievance against someone. Forgive as the Lord forgave you" Col 3:12-13

WRITNG YOUR OBITUARY

A time will come when someone will write your obituary. It might be a person who never met you or had even heard about you. What they write will be a compilation of what family members and friends recall at this time of stress. After a list of your progeny, there might be a list of positions you have held or where you worked along with any notable accomplishments.

But if you were to write your own obituary and had to write it today, what would you want to have included and what would you want to be emphasized? Each of us has a different view of self than anyone else including those closest to us. We know what is important to us and we know what we have done or intended to do but maybe didn't get around to getting done. The To Do list will probably not make your obituary even if you do write it yourself.

When you are gone, what impact will you have had on people, places and things? Did you live a happy life in which you made others around you happy? Will your departure sadden a number of people or won't people notice? Are there things you have started or strongly influenced that others might carry on to have a lasting effect? If you were to list the ten most important characteristics you have, what would they be? If you were to list the ten most important accomplishments of your life to date, what are they?

We are accountable to God for the life we have led. Romans 14:12 tells us, "So then each of will give an account of himself to God" (NKJV). Think about what we will tell God about our life when the time comes.

Reading this might prompt you to write your own obituary today based on your life so far. That could be helpful in at least two ways. One is that if you leave it with some loved ones they might be able to locate it when you are gone and use it as your actual obituary. More importantly, however, is that the writing of it might have an impact on you today. Is there a significant gap between the life that your vision includes and your actual life to date? What are the most important ways in which the two are different? Write them down on a list. Then make notations on the list about what you are currently doing in each area of activity. You are fortunate in that you are still alive and can impact how the obituary will read. If the obituary you would write today is not what you would like for it to be, what are you going to do today, tomorrow and next week about it?

STUDY QUESTIONS

1. Take the time to rough out what your obituary would look like if it were written today.
2. What are the ten most important characteristics that you hope others will see in you?
3. If there is a gap between where you are in life today and where you would like to be at life's end? What are you doing in the present to close that gap? 291

"Be wise in the way you act toward outsiders, make the most of every opportunity. Let your conversation be always full of grace, seasoned with salt, so that you might know how to answer everyone" Colossians 4:5-6

HOW WE ARE REMEMBERED

Have you ever thought about how you will be remembered? Some day each of us will die and one or more persons will stand up and say something about us. Have you thought about what will be said? Some comments will likely be about our personality, our activities and our accomplishments. Personality describes how we approach life and the people around us. Are we happy, positive, action oriented, like other people, find the best in them and help others, or would the opposites be described? Will people remember our smile or our grumpy look?

Our activities and our accomplishments will also be remembered. Which accomplishments are most likely to be mentioned about you? Will there be a long list from which to choose or will this section be eliminated while the speaker has to resort to generalities about how nice we were or talk about people related to us? What was important to us during our lifetime? What did we support and encourage?

We might also be remembered for the number of friends we had and how we treated others. Were we kind and considerate, loving, caring about others? What impact did we have on others, how many lives did we change for the good? Did people like us? Were we continually looking for ways to help others? Or were we self-centered and arrogant?

Our values including our Christian faith are more important than our personality or our accomplishments. What is important to us? What have we promoted, supported and encouraged? What do we believe in, including our faith? You might maintain that you are a Christian but John 13:34-35 states: "A new command I give you: Love one another. As I have loved you, so you must love one another. By this all men will know that you are my disciples, if you love one another."

Do you love one another with no exceptions? You must believe and you must love one another. Without this your Christian faith is not real. Will others be surprised that you claimed to be a Christian because of the way you treated other people? If your faith is real, will people remember you as a Christian? How will you be remembered?

STUDY QUESTIONS

1. How do you want to be remembered?
2. How would you feel if the world suddenly became aware of all of things you value (your value system)?
3. Will you be remembered for your last, worst act or will it be your last, Christian act?

283

"Let your conversation be without covetousness; and be content with such things as you have because God said, I will never leave you nor forsake you" Hebrews 13:5 KJV

"Then Judas Iscariot, one of the Twelve, went to the chief priests to betray Jesus to them. They were delighted to hear this and promised to give him money. So he watched for an opportunity to hand him over" Mark 14:10

RATIONALE FOR LIVING

Even if we haven't thought about it deeply, each of us has a rationale for living. How do we justify our existence? Do we contribute more back to this world than we use? If we have no plans for the future and if our goal when we wake up in the morning is to be comfortable, avoiding all pain while staying alive, and nothing more, then we live a simple, boring life. To this core of activities what would you add to fit your circumstance? Would it be to go to work, buy groceries, buy gas for the car and see some football on TV? Or maybe you would do all of those things but also have some bigger things in mind relating to family, going to work, buying groceries and getting the car fixed. Some of us like to hibernate in our shell.

Or maybe you would like to make a difference not only in your life but also in the lives of others. Maybe there are things you would like to accomplish, places you would like to visit and even characteristics of this world you would like to change as a result of your participation.

Most of us do have some future plans even if they are very fuzzy, unwritten, unshared with others and with little or no effort being exercised to reach those goals. Here are two principles to consider: 1. <u>The more specific goals are, the more likely they are to be reached</u>. 2. <u>Written goals tend to be more specific than ones we keep in our head</u>. Fuzzy, unwritten, unshared goals have about as much chance of taking place as winning the lottery. But most of us have some of these fuzzy goals.

Les Brown, in his book *Live Your Dreams*, talks about the excuses we use for not pursuing our goals, our dreams. Rationalization at times seems much easier than making an effort that could possibly fail. Any effort is a risk. Everyone needs to take some risks in order to reach where God wants them to be. Romans 8:28 tells us, "in all things God works for the good of those who love Him." What is good for those who love Him is something to be sought in Bible study, prayer and a period of time in thinking through what gifts God has given us and the messages we are receiving either directly from God or through other people as to how we can make a difference in this world in concert with God.

What is your rationale for living? Did God place you where you are for a reason? What might that reason be? Does your daily behavior relate closely to that reason? While most of us do not think very far into the future, there will be a time later when we will look back and think about what our life has been. Will what we see make sense? Will God be pleased with what we have done? We cannot change what we have and have not done in the past but we are in control of the future. In your rationale for living, what is your next step?

STUDY QUESTIONS

1. Are you drifting through life or do you have some plans for the rest of your life? Are those plans written out?
2. Read Romans 8:28. What does that mean to you for what will happen in the rest of your life?
3. What are the excuses mentioned by Les Brown that apply to you keeping you from having direction in your life?

269

"Blessed is the one who perseveres under trial because, having stood the test, that person will receive the crown of life that the Lord has promised to those who love Him" James 1:12

ACQUIRING WISDOM

The process of acquiring wisdom should be continuous. All of us face challenges in life that could be resolved by the application of wisdom. But often we apply emotion, habit and tradition or irrational thought to the situation instead. There are situations in which we lack the wisdom needed because we do not seek to have that wisdom and other times when we have the wisdom but choose instead to take a course that requires less thought or that fits our emotions of the moment. All situations have better outcomes when wisdom is at least part of the method of resolution.

How do we acquire wisdom? Examples of wisdom are all around us. We acquire wisdom when we are around wise people who are exercising their wisdom. We learn by seeing how they approach a challenge, how they analyze the options and how they make a decision. A person who makes many wise decisions takes a unique approach to life.

Another way to acquire wisdom is through reading including biographies of those recognized as being wise in some way. This could be a leader like Thomas Jefferson or a scientist like Thomas Edison or Albert Einstein. While none of them were perfect, they stood out in their use of wisdom to form meaningful conclusions.

Most of us have acquired wisdom from mothers and fathers who exhibited wisdom in raising us. They were likely the first to demonstrate wisdom in our lives. How did they show wisdom and what can we learn from their examples?

Then there is wisdom within us. As we approach a significant issue in our lives, we can stop to analyze the situation, develop alternative paths that might be taken and then reason through which possible path would make the most sense. We are capable of making wise decisions but it requires taking the time to think, to reason and carefully consider what would happen with each of the options we consider.

Finally, our greatest source of wisdom is the Bible. Here we have hundreds of examples of wisdom being displayed (and some examples of the lack of it).

Proverbs 4:7 tells us, "Wisdom is supreme; therefore get wisdom. Though it cost all you have, get understanding." Solomon was considered the wisest person on earth. Abraham showed wisdom in leading the people. Job faced great adversity but his problems did not keep him from remaining wise in his choices.

Each of us was created in God's image with the capacity for wisdom. While other solutions such as habit, emotion and what others are doing might require less time and less thinking, we should seek wisdom in all of our decisions. Doing so is pleasing to God.

STUDY QUESTIONS

1. When you face a difficult situation, do you follow the advice of James 1:5?
2. Identify five of the wisest persons you have ever known. What is it about them that put them on your list?
3. Could you acquire greater wisdom in your decisions?

286

"While all the people were listening, Jesus said to His disciples, 'Beware of the teachers of the law. They like to walk around in flowing robes and love to be greeted in the marketplaces and have the most important seats in the synagogues and the places of honor at banquets. They devour widows' houses and for a show make lengthy prayers. Such men will be punished most severely'" Luke 20:4547

WHAT WILL YOUR LEGACY BE?

Legacy is the effect we have after we are gone from the world we have touched. Most of us would like that legacy to be a positive impact on many people or a tremendous positive impact on a small number of people. King David spoke about his legacy in Psalm 112:1-3: "Praise the Lord. Blessed are those who fear the Lord, who find great delight in his commands. Their children will be mighty in the land; the generation of the upright will be blessed. Wealth and riches are in their houses, and their righteousness endures forever."

A legacy with a long-term positive impact has four parts: 1) our value (faith) system, 2) our gifts, talents, skills, intellect, education and experience, 3) our vision, mission and goals, and 4) our behavior (action) effectively utilizing the first three. So what are some of the things we can do now to ensure a positive legacy?

1) VALUES/FAITH The essence of who we are is in our values which includes our Christian faith. Clearly held values become significant when they really define us; that is, we hold them so intensely that all who have contact with us are aware of those values including our faith.

2) CAPABILITIES What gifts did God give us? We need to know and develop our gifts while finding ways to compensate for those we lack. Then, to develop these gifts, what are the skills, tools, education and experience we need to acquire as well as the support from other people and organizations we have now or will need to acquire?

3) VISION/MISSION/GOALS For a legacy to be remarkable, the vision, mission and goals must themselves be remarkable. The needed resources must be deftly combined in a timely, cost-effective manner that inspires others to also want to achieve the mission with intensity. It has often been said that those who do not achieve the legacy they seek are those who have not found what it takes to get along with other people and to lead a cohesive group toward commonly held objectives. When we effectively communicate our vision, mission and goals we encourage others to join in the pursuit of

them. Is the path to the vision, mission and goals clear in your mind even if not clear to others? Do you have the courage to go down that path?

4) ACTION An idea (vision) we conceive has no impact by itself, but in concert with carefully considered action, it can lead to a treasured legacy. Part of that action is in how we impact everyone around us. Does that impact contribute to the legacy we seek? Has our vision become our mission in life? We must demonstrate as Christians the desire to love one another.

Our Christian faith is the most important of our values and it will permeate our legacy which is not completed until we go to Heaven. A legacy is the picture that others have of us when we are gone. Make that legacy one that will positively impact the next two or more generations.

STUDY QUESTIONS

1. Write down five thoughts about what you would like to have others remember about you when you are gone.
2. Which of the four steps above are the most difficult for you to attain? Why is that?
3. Think of a person (possibly still living) whose legacy you admire. What is it that you admire?

376

CHAPTER FIVE

WISDOM AND OUR RELATIOSHIP TO SOCIETY/CULTURE

Treating Others, Forgiveness, Trusting, Being Relevant, People Liking You, Being Thankful, Being Politically Correct, Being God Correct, Being Altruistic, Servanthood, Not About Me, Role Models, Judging, Principle, Power, Position

WHAT WOULD THE WORLD BE LIKE IF EVERYONE SHARED MY VALUES, ATTITUDES AND BEHAVIOR?

Each one of us would have to answer this in our own way because we don't share the same values, attitudes and behavior. In another program, the emphasis was on how the major problems of the world come from the values and attitudes of some of the people who through arrogance, greed and selfishness create wars, famines, injustice and unhappiness for others.

Think about your own values, your own attitudes and your own behavior (which should be consistent with your values and attitudes). If the rest of the world shared those values, attitudes and behavior, would it be a much better world? Would we do away with crime, wars and other injustices in this world if the world were like you?

What are your values? What do you believe in? Do you believe in God? Do you accept the values that are advocated in the Bible? Do you value human life and human happiness? Do you believe that mankind is basically good or do you believe that everyone is at least partially dishonest and selfish and therefore you need to be that way in order to protect yourself? If others had your value system, would you feel safer in the world or feel the need for protection?

Then what about your attitudes? You can have the values Jesus talked about and still have a grumpy, sour attitude toward life and other people. Do you feel that others are picking on you or that they are ignoring you? Or is your attitude one in which you look each day for how to help some person or group in order to make this a happier and more just world?

Then your behavior? Normally we behave in accordance with our values and our attitudes. Does your temper, your laziness, your lack of courage, your lack of a sense of purpose cause you to behave in a manner that is inconsistent with a Godly set of values and attitudes?

Jesus wants us to be "...the salt of the earth..." and ... "the light of the world" (Matthew 5:13-14). Think about how the world would change if others were like you in values, attitudes and behavior. Would this be a better world?

STUDY QUESTIONS

1. Make a list of ten of your most important values.
2. Are your attitudes and behavior consistent with those values?
3. If most other people shared these values, would this be a better world? In what ways?

123

"Let us therefore come boldly unto the throne of grace, that we may obtain mercy, and find grace to help in time of need" Hebrews 4:16

"So that we may boldly say, The Lord is my helper, and I will not fear what man shall do unto me" Hebrews 13:6

"The best place to find a helping hand is at the end of your arm." Swedish proverb

"Dear children, do not let anyone lead you astray. He who does what is right is righteous." 1 John 3:7

"Every word of God is pure; He is a shield unto them who put their trust in Him" Proverbs 30:5 KJV

"We make a living by what we get, . . . but we make a life by what we give." Winston Churchill

BEING ALTRUISTIC

The dictionary definition of altruism is "the principle or practice of concern for the welfare of others. Altruism or selflessness is the opposite of selfishness." In human behavior, acting altruistically is contrasted with acting based on our ego. In simple terms, being altruistic means we are motivated more by what is good for others rather than what is good for me. In God's Plan for Service we have at times used the term being other-person centered for altruism. Jesus is our role model for acting altruistically.

When Jesus was asked, "which is the greatest commandment," he said,

> Love the Lord your God with all your heart and with all your soul and with all your mind. This is the first and greatest commandment. And the second is like it: Love your neighbor as yourself. All the Law and the Prophets hang on these two commandments." Matthew 22:37-40

When we love others we will want what is best for them and we will be willing to exert our efforts to ensure that their world will be what God's will is for them to the best of our ability. We can be Christians only by accepting this. Does this sound a lot like being altruistic? Altruism is the psychological term to describe what we know as Christian love. The true test of love and altruism is exhibited in our daily behavior.

If we are Christians, our challenge is how to exhibit altruism each day. Here are a few challenging thoughts. How often when you speak or write do you begin the sentence with I? When in a conversation, how often do you seek to show an interest in the other person in contrast to talking about yourself? When you think about how you will spend a block of time, to what extent is your interest in serving others compared to what pleases you? If you have a To Do list, how many of the items on the list could be considered to be altruistic? When you greet others, is your first thought to tell them what you have done and what they could do for you or what you can do for them? When you do something for someone else, to what extent do you think about the long-term impact for that person instead of how great you are for what you have done? Do you share with others what is in your bank account?

Being altruistic means being generous with all you have that could benefit others. This includes our financial assets and our possessions in addition to our time. Look at your checkbook or credit card statement. How many items listed there could have a possible benefit for others, not just yourself? Being altruistic is an attitude of love for others as Jesus displayed in His love for others. Jesus showed love for those he met and not just those close to Him. Jesus used the parable of the Good Samaritan to illustrate the point. When we exhibit love for others, we will want to share what we have as well as do what we can physically.

Think about the extent to which you are following the commandment of Jesus in Matthew 22. Jesus said, "Love your neighbor as yourself." That is sometimes hard to do when a person or group stands for what the New Testament describes as a sin or the person or group has exhibited a dislike for us. This requires energy and sometimes money and courage. Do you love your neighbor as Jesus commanded? Would other people describe you as being altruistic?

STUDY QUESTIONS

1. How altruistic (selflessness) would you describe yourself on a scale of 1-10 with ten being the most altruistic?
2. Give three descriptions in which you have been altruistic. Make one of them something you physically did for someone, one in which you gave money that benefitted others and one in which your possessions were of benefit to others.
3. Read the Scripture again from Matthew quoted above. What does it say to you?

189A

WHAT IS SERVANTHOOD?

Servanthood is the art and practice of being an effective servant. We tend to think of being a servant as being a lowly state with low pay and low esteem by others in society. However, Jesus said (Matthew 20:26-27), "...whoever wants to become great among you must be your servant, and whoever wants to be first must be your slave" (servant). So this means that if we want earthly success, instead of seeking power and authority, we should seek to be a servant.

Jesus was our role model as a servant. Mt 20:28 records Jesus as saying, "Just as the Son of Man did not come to be served, but to serve, and to give His life as a ransom for many." There can be no greater role as a servant than to give one's life. In Philippians 2:7 Jesus Christ is described as having "made himself nothing by taking the very nature of a servant." An outstanding example of servanthood was recorded by Luke (1:38) where he quotes Mary, the Mother of Jesus, as saying, "I am the Lord's servant . . . May your word to me be fulfilled."

What are we to do as a servant? John 12:26 records Jesus as saying, "Whoever serves me must follow me; and where I am, my servant also will be. My Father will honor the one who serves me." Think about that statement. "Where I am, my servant also will be." So when we find Jesus Christ, that is where we are also to be. Jesus Christ took on the "very nature of a servant." This means being devoted to service to others. Jesus offered us salvation, eternal life in Heaven. There is no greater gift. Yet in His life on earth, he modeled servanthood, the every day behavior dedicated to serving others, even when the world He was serving rebuked him.

You might be thinking, how would I make things happen as a servant? Robert Greenleaf in his essay *Servant as Leader* said, "The servant-leader is servant first. It begins with the natural feeling that one wants to serve, to serve first. Then conscious choice brings one to aspire to lead. That person is sharply different from one who is *leader* first. . . . The leader-first and the servant-first are two extreme types." A servant-leader seeks to empower others and through this the whole organization is lifted.

This brings us to thinking about how each of us could be a servant. To be a servant requires an attitude that says that we love others and we want the best for them. We add the willingness to exert our own energy to secure what is best for them. The opportunities are boundless whether in our own family, our friends, those we see everyday or complete strangers. One final thought from Scripture, 2 Timothy 2:24 tells us: "And the Lord's servant must not be quarrelsome but must be kind to everyone, able to teach, not resentful." Servanthood requires no further preparation. It can start now.

STUDY QUESTIONS:

1. How would you define servanthood?
2. What is your attitude toward others? Do you receive satisfaction from serving others?
3. Think of three ways that Jesus was a servant to others.

204

3 John 11: "Dear friend, do not imitate what is evil but what is good."

"Let another man praise you, and not your own mouth; a stranger but not thine own lips" Proverbs 27:2 KJV

TRUSTING OTHERS

Who do you trust and how do you determine whether another person is trustworthy? We trust others based on our assessment of their current behavior and how we predict they will act in the future. We measure their behavior against our values, values that tell us what a trustworthy person is like. What are some of those values? They include honesty, forthrightness, dependability, truthfulness and reputation. There are non-verbal characteristics as well such as shifting eyes, failure to make eye contact and poor treatment of others. Some people, sometimes known as con men, are good at giving the right impression in the short term but their actions eventually show them to be not worthy of trust.

To look at it from the opposite direction, what about people trusting you? Do you feel that most people trust you from the time that they meet you and continue to do so over a period of time as they get to know you? What are the characteristics you have that cause others to trust you? These are characteristics to cherish, to protect and ensure that they continue to be an essential part of who you are.

When we don't trust others or others don't trust us, we are kept from accomplishing some of what we have set out to do. When trust is lacking, we tend to set up safeguards to protect us. These safeguards slow down action and can make action more expensive or more complex. It could even cause an effort to fail.

So how do we protect ourselves from untrustworthy people? Unless we are in an emergency and have no other choices, don't deal with a person you do not trust. What appears to be a great deal with an untrustworthy person is likely to turn out to be a disaster. Be willing to turn away from a situation that is very tempting by dealing only with trustworthy people.

At the same time, we must be sure that we exemplify trustworthiness in our behavior so that others will want to relate to us. Think about the characteristics you possess. Remember that people liking you is not the same as people trusting you. Remember too that we should not expect others to trust us when we find it difficult to trust others.

One of the best pathways to obtain the trust of others is to demonstrate the fruits of the Spirit as Paul outlines in Galatians 5:22: "love, joy, peace, patience, kindness, goodness, faithfulness, gentleness and self-control." Which of these characteristics do others see as how they would describe <u>you</u>?

STUDY QUESTIONS

1. Trusting others must have balance. We cannot trust everyone but we must trust many. Where are you on this balance?
2. Which of the characteristics in Galatians 5:22 fits you?
3. Why do people trust you? 103

"May the God of hope fill you with all joy as you trust in Him, so that you may overflow with hope by the power of the Holy Spirit" Romans 15:13

"He who trusts in his own heart is a fool: but whoso walketh wisely, he shall be delivered" Proverbs 19:26 KJV

HOW WE TREAT OTHERS

Poor treatment of others suggests that <u>we</u> have a poor self-concept – one that is out of balance in terms of ego, human values, potential, accomplishment and human relationships, as well as our relationship to God.

When we <u>do</u> treat others with kindness, respect, honor and integrity, it suggests some good things about <u>us</u>. Let's look at some of those characteristics that must exist in us in order for us to treat others with kindness, respect, honor and integrity.

1. We must have a healthy, realistic self-concept. When we don't like ourselves, we won't like anyone else either. A healthy self-concept is one that has achieved balance between arrogance at one extreme and self-pity at the other. A realistic self-concept is one that is tied to actual accomplishments and ability to perform. However, the more we accomplish, the more likely we are to think we are greater than we are. Our self-concept must be kept in balance.

2. A healthy self-concept will recognize the supremacy of God. We will find joy in serving and praising God and, through God, serving others. We will see ourselves as a creature of God and will have joy in our hearts.

3. We will treat others well if we also see them as the children of God and his creatures. We will see the worth of others. We will find joy in the accomplishments of others and not feel that any gain by others is a cost to us.

4. We will set goals in this life but they will be goals to be the best that we can be in whatever we set out to do. We will not set goals to simply do more than others. Our own Christian excellence is defined by the gifts, talents, education and experience we have come to possess. We will seek our potential and not to overcome others.

Do these four characteristics sound difficult to attain? It all begins with our attitude in life. The most important attitude has been defined by Jesus as recorded in Matthew 22:37-39: "…Love the Lord your God with all your heart and with all your soul and with all your mind... And the second is like it: Love your neighbor as yourself."

Start with loving God, loving others and having a healthy respect for self. Then set some goals that reflect your potential. Smile and find joy in life. You will find yourself treating others well.

STUDY QUESTIONS

1. Write down some notes that come to mind as you think of your own self-concept.
2. Look over these notes. What patterns or characteristics are prevalent?
3. What kind of shape is your Christian faith in? Is it vibrant? Are you actively worshipping God? Is God number one in your life?

162

"My dream is of a place and a time where America will once again be seen as the last best hope on earth." Abraham Lincoln

"Every person in this life has something to teach me – and as soon as I accept that, I open myself to truly listening." Catherine Doucette

"He who trusts in his own heart is a fool: but whoso walketh wisely, he shall be delivered" Proverbs 19:26 KJV

HOW MANY FRIENDS DO YOU HAVE?

A person who was interviewing for a job in a distant city asked the person hosting the interview, will I have any friends here? The response was, how many friends do you have now? If you don't have any now, you won't have any here either.

C S Lewis, in writing about the four loves of mankind, makes a clear distinction between companions and friends. Friends are the persons you gravitate toward, who you seek out, who you enjoy spending time with, who bring you happiness. A companion is a person you know, maybe even for a long time, but a person in whom you would not confide your deeper thoughts. A companion might even be a person you admire, you enjoy as a co-worker, but is still not a friend.

So what makes someone a friend? A friend is a person we share interests and thoughts with, a person with whom we might carry on either a light or a deep conversation, a person you might both laugh with in a time of joy and cry with in a moment of sorrow. We enjoy our friends and we count on them to be there when we need them. They give us happiness in that we know that they care about us just as we care about them and what is important to them. A friend is a person from whom we expect nothing except friendship. If you expect something else, like a great deal in a purchase, that isn't friendship.

A man can have female friends and a woman can have male friends. In writing this, I sat down to count my friends. I came up with 16 but your number could be fewer or more. There is no ideal number. The significance is that we have some friends. Friendships can cross many boundaries. None of my friends has had the same career. A minority of them attend the same Church. Some have been friends since high school while others have become friends more recently.

The old adage is that to have friends you must first be a friend. What are you doing to extend the hand of friendship to others? Do you introduce yourself to others and show an interest in them? Each of us should be a candidate for becoming someone's friend. What are you doing to cultivate new friends as well as keeping in contact with old friends?

STUDY QUESTIONS

1. Have you added friends over the past five years? How did you meet these new friends?
2. What are you doing to "be a friend" to others? Extending oneself to others might not result in an ongoing friendship but it does help bring happy and peaceful relationships.
3. How many of your neighbors do you know and had a conversation with them in the past year?

92

"Rejoice in the Lord always. I will say it again: Rejoice! Let your gentleness be evident to all. The Lord is near. Do not be anxious about anything, but in everything, by prayer and petition, with thanksgiving, present your requests to God" Philippians 4:4-7

"Looking unto Jesus the author and finisher of our faith, who for the joy that was set before Him endured the cross, despising the shame, and is set down at the right hand of the throne of God" Hebrews 12:2 KJV

"Who is wise and understanding among you? Let him show it by his good life, by deeds done in the humility that comes from wisdom" James 3:13

TOMMY, BRIAN, TOM AND DAVID

This is a short story about Tommy, Brian, Tom and David. If we are fortunate we have people in our lives who serve as role models for the rest of us. Often we are uncertain of how to act, so it helps us to have role models around us. I am very fortunate in that I have a number of them in my life but for this story I have picked out only four of them. This story could have a sequel with others as role models. What makes these four my role models?

Consistent and earnest behavior of an individual tells us what values rest inside of the person. All are Christians who follow the teaching in Proverbs 4:5: "Get wisdom, get understanding." We can admire these values in others. We wish they might be more present in us. Values determine behavior. It is the behavior that comes from these values we see whenever we encounter a person. Let's look at some of these behaviors.

The most pervasive behavior of these four is that they are other-person centered. Every encounter with others is about the other person. They look for ways to serve others either through another person, a service organization, a church, or directly with that person. They meet their responsibilities happily. They are involved in community projects that benefit all of us. They sincerely desire to make this a better society. They do it not because they must but because they enjoy brightening the lives of other people. Once you know them, you realize that if you needed their help, all you would need to do is ask.

They brighten the days of others through a cheerful countenance, through greeting others, through concern when appropriate and a helping hand when needed. They make an effort to get to know others. They seek to learn from others. They find a way to brighten the day of other people.

The four role models are people of integrity. It means when they say something there is no reason to doubt it. Their word is solid gold. They are confident people who are not taken in by those who make the loudest noise. They stand firm on their principles. One of their principles is their Christian faith. They have numerous friends because they have <u>been</u> a friend to many.

They are people who have goals, who set out to accomplish something important in life and have the discipline to see it through. They enlist others to work with them rather than running over others to reach their own goals.

Who are these people? Look around you for a Tommy, Brian, Tom or David. How many role models do you see? Do they have many of these same characteristics? Do they brighten your life?

STUDY QUESTIONS

1. Is there a Tommy, Brian, Tom or David in your inner circle of friends? How did that happen?
2. What can you learn from people like Tommy, Brian, Tom and David?
3. Are you a role model for others? How many of the characteristics described above would others see in you?

261

"His divine power has given us everything we need for life and godliness through our knowledge of Him who called us by His own glory and goodness" 2 Peter 1:3

CHOOSE MENTORS WISELY

Let's explore the concept of having a mentor and choosing wisely when selecting that mentor. A mentor is a person or group who provides counsel, advice, support and friendship to a person who is open to receiving such counsel for the issues of life or in guidance on a specific area of life. A mentor might be utilized in a time of dire need but is also an important element in planning the future by guiding a person through the challenges and opportunities each of us faces. A mentor does not replace our relationship with God but might serve as God's agent on earth in guiding us. Each of us can benefit from having one or more mentors as we face personal, career, family, health and other issues. We could have multiple mentors with one dealing with career issues and another for personal or faith issues for example.

But how do we find such a person or persons? Part of choosing a mentor wisely is to determine what knowledge or experience would make the person helpful to us. It must be established whether this mentor is for career, family/personal or other issues. They are not likely to be the same person.

A suitable mentor is usually older with more experience in career and life, well grounded in his or her Christian faith and usually but not always of the same gender (less important with career than personal issues). Looking around us might identify such a person if we look for the criteria and not just how we normally see this person. Another option is to talk with a trusted friend, pastor or church leader to learn of possibilities not currently known to us. A famous or well-known person is highly unlikely to be suitable. Close friends might not be objective and too prone to giving advice based on what they think you should do.

Once you talk with a potential mentor and they begin by telling you what to do, you probably have the wrong person. A helpful mentor will listen so as to understand your situation and what you want to accomplish. A suitable mentor will ask you questions rather than telling you what to do. The questions will be directed to helping you clarify the situation and the options you face by making you think. A mentor should help you understand the decisions you need to make rather than making decisions for you. Meetings with a mentor could be a long-term relationship with periodic meetings, an annual event or a single encounter. If necessary due to distance, it could be by telephone or email.

Solomon, considered the wisest man to have ever lived, even recognized the importance and value of a mentor. He said the following in Proverbs 15:22-23: "Plans fail for lack of counsel, but with many advisers they succeed. A man finds joy in giving an apt reply – and how good is a timely word!" "Use your intelligence, your experience, and your common sense: choose a mentor with wisdom, compassion and vision. Look for someone you respect, someone who will inspire" (*Make the Most of You* by Patrick Lindsay). Consider also how you might be a mentor to others.

STUDY QUESTIONS

1. Do you think you could use a mentor? In what aspects of your life could a mentor be useful to you?
2. Are you already a mentor? How do you mentor in comparison to what is described above?
3. In selecting a mentor, it is not advisable to approach him or her to ask if they would be your mentor. Start with some of the questions on your mind to see how they respond without mentioning mentors. How they respond will tell you whether they would be suitable. What questions might you ask a potential mentor to discover whether they might be suitable?

322

"But someone will say, 'You have faith, I have deeds.' Show me your faith without deeds, and I will show you my faith by what I do. You believe that there is one God. Good! Even the demons believe that – and shudder" James 2:18-19

INVESTING IN OTHERS

We invest in many things: a house, a car, clothing, hobbies, vacations. But how much do we invest in the lives of other people? Investment means taking something we have and utilizing it to assist some other entity. What we have is time, talent, money and opportunity.

Probably the most often used excuse for not investing in others is that we are too busy. Yet when we look at volunteer activities in the church and the community, we find many very busy people. Busy people get a lot done by planning their time and setting priorities among their obligations and their opportunities to serve others. Busy people take care of their families including their extended family, have time for friends and relaxation, take care of their health, are active in their church and still have time for others.

When we say we are too busy, what is it that we are so busy doing? Is the real reason that we are busy focusing on things for ourselves? Or could it be that we are afraid if we offer to help, we could be rejected? Or maybe if we offer to help others, we won't know how to do what is needed or that it will cost us some money? It could be that we are concerned about the time that helping others will take away from our leisure time and we aren't willing to part with that luxury.

Those who find the time, the talent, the money or the opportunity tend to find that investing in others is very rewarding. There might not be a thank you for every thing that we do, but people generally appreciate what is done for them. Investing time with a group at a local elementary school will have the reward in the children's eyes as you assist them with a story or help them solve a math problem or how to write a sentence. There might even be a few hugs. Helping seniors who need meals brought to them is rewarding when you see their situation and how the meal is essential to their well-being. Most volunteer work does not require any expenditure of money but it does require some time. It can be scheduled to fit your time requirements.

Even if we are too busy and the rewards of helping others are not important to us, as Christians we are told to "Love one another" (John 13:34). If we love one another, we will want to invest time, energy and money in helping others. What might you do to show love for others by investing in them this week?

STUDY QUESTIONS

1. Give an example of how you have invested in the life of another person through time, money, talent, energy or opportunity.
2. What are the opportunities around you currently for investing in the lives of others?
3. As you consider the rest of your life, who or what needs an investment of your time, money and energy? Can't come up with anything? What about your Church? 358

"If we deliberately keep on sinning after we have received the knowledge of the truth, no sacrifice for sins is left, but only a fearful expectation of judgment and of raging fire that will consume the enemies of God" Hebrews 10:26-27

"There is no better way to convince others than first to convince self." Cicero (186-43 BC)

"The wealth of the wise is their crown, but the folly of fools yields folly." Proverbs 14:24

"Wisdom reposes in the heart of the discerning and even among fools she lets herself be known." Proverbs 14:33

ROLE MODELS

Role models are the people who have had a profound impact on our lives by being the person who was or is in a position to have a profound impact on others by living out a role by worthy of emulation. The Bible extols the benefit of having a role model. Solomon said, in Proverbs 13:20: "Walk with the wise and become wise, for a companion of fools suffers harm."

The ultimate role model for all of us is Jesus Christ. The Son of God came to earth and lived without blemish providing an excellent role model in every aspect of His life. By reading the New Testament we can find multiple examples of how Jesus Christ served as the ultimate role model.

Each of us has had positive role models in those who have lived among us. They have positively impacted us. Some people have impacted us only in a small aspect of our lives but in an important way. Others have had a broad impact on us.

When another person has a broad impact on our lives, what are the ways in which that is shown? Maybe the most important is in how they have impacted our own self-perception, how we see ourselves. Our self-perception is key to the utilization of the talents, gifts, education and experience we possess. If we doubt ourselves, all of our capabilities can be severely limited. If we don't think we can do something, we probably can't. Role models can help us to believe in ourselves and thus increase the positive impact we can have on others and society around us.

A second area in which a role model can have considerable impact on us is the decision making process. Remember WWJD? What would Jesus do? We can reflect on how our role models would handle situations we find ourselves facing.

A third area in which a role model can have considerable impact on us is in how to relate to other people. Role models in my life have excelled in this and have helped me to modify my behavior to become more other person centered.

Fourth, a positive role model with a major impact is a person who affects how we think and what we think about. In doing so, we are likely to be challenged to be a different person. We become a different person as a result of our relationship with this person.

As we gain experience, education and perspective, we can be a role model to others. For some people, we likely already are role models. Think about how to increase your effect as a role model to others.

At the risk of missing some person outside of my family who has served as a major role model for me, I have identified eight men. One of them is still living and all impacted me for a year or more. They have been Ralph Strouf and John Halmond of North Muskegon, MI, Howard Altman of Dade City, FL, Henry Richardson of Havre de Grace, MD, Dr. Donald Luck of New Cumberland, PA, Dr. Don Atkinson of Franklin, TN, Dr. Henry Webb of Johnson City, TN and Dr. Bryce Jessup of Rocklin, CA. Two have been my teachers, three have been friends, and three have been professional colleagues. Who are the positive role models with a broad impact on your life?

STUDY QUESTIONS

1. In addition to those role models who have had a broad impact on our lives, there are people who might have had a momentary impact (a minute or even months) on us. Who might some of those people be in your life?
2. Who in your family has impacted your life? In what ways?
3. Who are the major impact people who have been role models for you?

186

"This is the assurance we have in approaching God: that if we ask anything according to His will, He hears us" 1 John 5:14

FEELING VALUED BY OTHERS

A friend of mine, who also happens to be on the Board of Directors of God's Plan for Service, read our program about being a good listener. His comment was "Ouch." He went on to say, "I love to talk but I'll admit I am a lousy listener (How did I make it in sales for 40 years?). It also reminded me of a few of my daily readings this year in 'Jesus Calling.' I know it's most important that we LISTEN for the Lord's voice in our life/ lives." This same person spends time visiting prisoners to hear their stories, provide encouragement and help them with Bible study. I reflected on his comment for some time and concluded that one of the reasons why he was so successful "in sales for forty years" is because he has the gift of helping people to FEELING VALUED BY OTHERS, our current topic.

All of us enjoy feeling that someone with whom we are communicating values (cares) about who we are, what we do, what we think and the impact we have on others. Think about how that impacts you. The people we enjoy being around are people who care (show value) concerning us. In turn, the people we care about the most are people we seek out and enjoy time with on a frequent basis. We value them and everything about them. That might be a spouse, children or grandchildren but it also includes the people we consider to be our friends.

When we feel valued by others, what are some of the things that we sense? Here is a partial list. Basic to the list is

1. **Caring, loving.** All of us want to be loved even if we have difficulty showing this. We want people to care about us. As Christians we will want to care about and love others. 1 John 3:18 reads "Dear children, let us not love with words or speech but with actions and in truth." It must be genuine, and show itself in action. "This is how we know that we belong to the truth..." (v. 9)
2. **Enjoying time with others.** I have another friend with whom I have lunch often without an agenda. We just enjoy each other's company.
3. **Enjoying things about us**, characteristics and interests we have, our willingness to listen to them talk about what is important in their lives.

4. **Smiling.** When two people who care about one another see each other, we are likely to smile. A smile reflects happiness, openness, caring, loving.

5. **Enjoying hearing about things that we are doing,** have done or plan to do. This includes our successes, illnesses, events, new thoughts or perspectives. In turn, we want to hear about things that they are doing.

A person I met some years ago made the comment in a conversation, that a good conversationalist is the person who asks about <u>you</u> based on a genuine interest and only talks about self when asked. We demonstrate our love and caring about others in finding ways in which we can enrich their lives, bring them closer to God and help to understand John 14:6. When we focus on ourselves we are not following the example of Jesus. When we focus on others, our own lives become richer, happier and more fulfilled. It also brings us closer to God. What might you be able to do this week to focus on helping people you greet to feel that others value them?

STUDY QUESTION

1. Count up the number of people you can identify by name you might have helped to have the feeling of being valued by others.
2. Is there a person among those with whom you associate that you have found difficult to demonstrate caring about? Is it because of that person, the circumstances or is it you?
3. Do you have a success story? Describe it.

365

"May our Lord Jesus Christ himself and God our Father, who loved us and by His grace gave us eternal encouragement and good hope, encourage your hearts and strengthen you in every good deed and word" 2 Thessalonians 2:16

BEING RELEVANT TO OTHERS

Are you relevant to others? The writer Pam Holloway once made the comment that "We become relevant in the lives of others when we learn about their interests, wants and needs."

Lucius Seneca, Roman stoic philosopher whose life coincided with the life of Jesus Christ, is credited with the statement:

> No man can live happily who regards himself alone, who turns everything to his own advantage. Thou must live for another if thou wishes to live for thyself.

When you talk with another person, whether friend or a person you have just met, how much of that conversation is made up of you talking about you? Almost every person enjoys the circumstance when someone else shows an interest in him or her as an individual. When you talk with this person, you have the opportunity to engage them in talking about who they are. When you do so, you will learn and you find some things very interesting. If you insist in talking only about yourself, remember that you already know about yourself so you are not learning anything by just listening to yourself ramble on. We become more interesting to others when we learn from others and situations we encounter in life. Many others are relevant to us in turn. We need to seek them out to enrich our lives from our encounter with them.

Returning to Seneca's advice, he said we need to get beyond turning "things to our own advantage" or focusing on ourselves in order to, as Seneca put it, "to live for thyself." He is saying that real satisfaction in life does not come from concentrating upon oneself. Instead, he is saying that real satisfaction in life comes from living for others. This other-person centeredness can lead us to satisfaction that comes from seeing the life of another person enhanced by something we have done or said.

Jesus Christ was relevant to the lives of the people around him but many of them did not know it and resisted his impact. Because he was so relevant, though, his influence grew even after he left his physical time here through followers who understood that relevancy. Now virtually everyone has the opportunity to learn and accept his relevancy. Jesus also told us how to be relevant to others in Matthew where after saying the greatest commandment was to "Love the Lord your God with all your heart" (Mt 22:37), he added, "And the second is like it: Love your neighbor as yourself" (Mt 22:39).

Think about the many opportunities you have today to do something for another person or group, to be relevant to them. What are you going to do today to follow Seneca's advice and do something for someone else? Think about how Jesus Christ was relevant then and now. Are you relevant in the lives of others?

STUDY QUESTIONS

1. Look at Pam Holloway's advice above. How does this apply to you?
2. In what ways might Seneca's advice make sense for your life?
3. List at least three things you have done in the past twenty-four hours that made you "relevant to others."

231

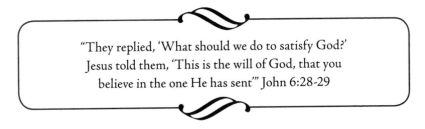

"They replied, 'What should we do to satisfy God?'
Jesus told them, 'This is the will of God, that you
believe in the one He has sent'" John 6:28-29

CHOOSING BATTLES CAREFULLY

We all face conflict from time to time but we should choose our battles carefully. While most conflicts we face in life are minor battles, they still interrupt the positive flow of life. Many of these conflicts are within us as we consider a decision for personal action. The battles or conflicts we are talking about today, however, are those when we find ourselves in conflict with another person or group.

When we find ourselves in a conflict with others, we have two major choices. One is to walk away and attempt to ignore the conflict. Sometimes this works. The other is to engage in the conflict. Not all conflicts are acrimonious. The conflict might be an error in your bank account resolved with a call to your bank.

Most conflicts involve our emotions even when internal for us. Establishing fault and what each person has said or done is central to the conflict. Should you become involved or walk away?

Choosing battles carefully means knowing when to pursue the issue and when to walk away. Choosing to do battle is appropriate in the following circumstances:

1. When it involves your Christian faith or some other principle that guides your life. Stand your ground for a principle but remember that most conflicts are based on a preference, not a principle.
2. When the outcome really matters such as an issue with a long-term impact or has a legal implication.
3. Patrick Lindsay stated: "Some battles are not worth the energy and can leave both sides losers." Is it worth the energy? Can there be a winner?

When your day is not going as well as you wish, you can blame other people or circumstances and thus create a conflict. You can avoid most of these conflicts by not creating it. Accept responsibility for your own errors or other failures to do what is expected of you or what you expect of yourself.

We have preferences which might be different from the preferences of others. Wisdom helps us decide when to stand our ground for a preference. Some people love to be in conflict. Don't let such people draw you into a conflict. By giving in on some issues, we win the larger issue by being the compromiser and showing compassion for others. We can choose to be in conflict most of the time or we can lead a life in which we carefully choose our battles and live a more peaceful life. Sometimes peace is preferable to being proven right. Jesus, in fact, stated: "Blessed are the peacemakers for they will be called children of God" (Matthew 5:9). Jesus stood his ground with the money changers in the temple but most of the time he elected to exemplify love for others as in the parable of the woman at the well. Jesus chose his battles carefully. Each of us should do no less.

STUDY QUESTIONS

1. When you disagree with someone, are you always right? How important is it to be proven that you are right and someone else is wrong?
2. Under what circumstances would you walk away from an interpersonal conflict?
3. Think about a personal conflict that you had that was based on principle (including your Christian faith) and another conflict that was based on preference. Did you handle the two situations differently?

323

"And now, through Christ, all the kindness of God has been poured out upon us undeserving sinners and how He is sending us out around the world to tell all people everywhere the great thing God has done for them, so that they, too, will believe and obey Him" Romans 1:5

JUDGING OTHERS

Romans 14:1 reads "Accept the one whose faith is weak, without quarreling over disputable matters." Paul had many reasons to pass judgment on others based on the way he had been treated in various cities during his missionary journeys. Yet he is instructing his readers (probably Jewish Christians in Rome) to refrain from judgment of others. We might wonder what "disputable matters" would include. The NIV commentary explains, "Christians do not agree on all matters pertaining to the Christian life, nor do they need to." At the same time, there are many teachings in the Bible that are very clear on which there can be no dispute.

After reminding the reader "Christ died and returned to life so that he might be the Lord of both the dead and the living" (Romans 14:9) (all Christians), Paul said, "You, then, why do you judge others? Or why do you treat them with contempt? For we will all stand before God's judgment seat" (Romans 14:10). In verse 13 Paul adds, "Therefore let us stop passing judgment on one another. Instead, make up your mind not to put any stumbling block or obstacle in the way of others."

Possibly some of you reading this have been part of a church which either split or was in heated debate over "disputable matters." This is a sorry state when Christians hold to a position in Christian life over which they are willing to destroy God's church. Having been a member of a number of churches in various cities over the years, I have yet to see a church divided over the essentials of the Christian faith. All divisions I have seen have been over "disputable matters" as Paul called it in which persons or groups were asserting that their interpretation of the Christian life or value of the pastor was the correct one and that their church brother had it wrong to the point of not wanting to worship together with that brother. When we reach that point, we sin.

We are likely to find it tempting to reach conclusions that we become entrenched in to the point of declaring that any other conclusion is wrong with anger justifiable over the issue. Church boards are likely to include different opinions on "disputable matters" but because Christians are to love one another (see 1 John 2:5-11), we must find ways to compromise, to seek common ground as we maintain the mission of the Church. Paul concludes this thought in Romans 14:19 with, "Let us therefore make every effort to do what leads to peace and to mutual edification." If we weigh each of our opinions against "peace and mutual edification" as well as to love, Christians should be able to reason together to make decisions that will be pleasing to God. Are you willing to listen to reason and to love without judging others rather than holding fast to your opinions on "disputable matters?"

STUDY QUESTIONS

1. Read all of Romans 14 and 1 John 2. Reflect on the messages they have for you. What is the most important concept that you draw from these passages?
2. Are you clear on what Paul meant by "disputable matters?"
3. Are you judging other Christians on some "disputable matter?"

366

"Do not judge, and you will not be judged. Do not condemn, and you will not be condemned. Forgive, and you will be forgiven. Give, and it will be given to you. A good measure pressed down, shaken together and running over, will be poured into your lap. For with the measure you use, it will be measured to you." Luke 6:38-39

"At this moment I have a heart of prayer. As I have assumed my duties, I humbly pray to Almighty God in the words of King Solomon: 'Therefore give to Your servant an understanding heart to judge Your people, that I might discern between good and evil. For who is able to judge this great people of yours.'"
President Harry S. Truman upon assuming office, 1945

REMEMBER THOSE IN PRISON

Please remember those in prison. The Scripture comes from the Book of Hebrews (13:1-3 NIV-MIT):

> Keep on loving each other as brothers. Do not forget to entertain strangers, for by so doing some people have entertained angels without knowing it. Remember those in prison as if you were fellow prisoners, and those who are mistreated as if you yourselves were suffering.

Most people have never visited a prison, entertained strangers or reached out to a person who has been mistreated. Why is that? Part of the reason is that there are few avenues by which we might do any of these acts of Christian love. Rescue missions and some churches provide a bed and breakfast for homeless people while providing Christian messages. It was common in our early history to entertain strangers; the inns that existed were sometimes dangerous places. Organizations such as Prison Fellowship help to bring the Christian message to prisoners. Various governments and Christian agencies bring food, shelter and medical care to the poor and mistreated. But all of these efforts involve only a very small percentage of adults. We have opportunities to assist in these efforts by financial contributions but even though this is relatively easy to do, how many people contribute to such organizations?

The ministry of God's Plan for Service includes reaching out to prisoners. One of our Board members visits several prisons on a regular basis. Three inmates of state prisons (it was five before two were released) receive the GPS message each week through the Post Office with a personal note attached. We have visited three of them in prison. But many prisoners receive no visitors and prisons closely regulate the list of those accepted as a visitor. The Gideons have a program of handing out Bibles and New Testaments to any prisoner who asks for one. But the fact remains that very few of us have any contact at all with strangers, prisoners or those who are mistreated.

Note that the writer of Hebrews puts all of this under the heading of "Keep on loving each other as brothers" (and sisters). Love and concern for others is the common denominator. Jesus commanded us to love one another (John 13:34). James 2:8 reads, "If you really keep the royal law found in Scripture, 'Love your neighbor as yourself,' you are doing right." One of the prisoners we serve told of a time when he went to an elderly lady next door whose yard was unkempt and offered to cut her grass. This is what the Book of Hebrews means by loving your neighbor.

James takes this to the step beyond loving your neighbor. James 2:14 (NIV-MIT) reads, "What good is it, my bothers, if a man claims to have faith but has no deeds? Can such faith save him?" James goes on to say that, "faith without deeds is useless" (James 2:20). While our salvation is not guaranteed by our deeds, if we have faith we will want to do as Jesus has commanded us. If we lack the desire to serve others, our faith is dead. How alive is your faith? What are you doing to serve others including strangers, prisoners and the mistreated? What is the church you attend doing to serve the mistreated, prisoners and strangers? Are you willing to share your time, talent and treasure to serve others in need?

STUDY QUESTIONS

1. Is there a person of whom you are aware who is in prison, in the military stationed away from home or a missionary in a far away place who would enjoy a letter from you?
2. Jesus commanded that we love our neighbor. Write down some evidence that you have shown agape love toward someone outside of your extended family.
3. If you were committed to prison for something you did not do, how would being in prison affect you?

408

THE NEXT PERSON YOU MEET

Later today or tomorrow there will be The Next Person You Meet. The person might be someone you know or a person you are meeting for the first time. We can be sure that this person has some problems, some challenges. The person might feel they have their challenges under control but all of us tend to have some doubts about whether some issue will turn out the way that we want it to. Some of these problems or challenges are private to them so that they don't want to share but often there are open issues. There might even be a desire to have someone to listen to what is on the person's mind.

When this person encounters you, they don't want you to add to their issues. So what can you do to ensure that you lighten the load rather than add to it? What you <u>can</u> do is smile, be kind and show an interest in the individual by letting them know that you care about them. Showing this interest doesn't have to be a statement to that effect. It could take the form of a smile, a handshake, a pat on the back or a simple comment that is implying love and concern. A comment such as 'How is it going?' might provide the opening that they are looking for to tell you some of what is on their mind.

So what do you do, then, if the person really unloads on you with tears and despair? The best thing to do is to listen. If in public, find a more discreet place such as a booth in a restaurant or just off to the side of other activities. Let the person know you care by listening without advice. Saying you had the issue too but worse will only drive them away. Ask simple questions that will help to clarify the situation. If special help is needed, you can offer to help them find that help. After understanding a good share of the challenge they are facing, you could make some suggestions for a next step. Don't pretend that you fully understand, particularly when the person with the issue probably doesn't understand it fully either. As you conclude this conversation, try to get the person to articulate a positive next step that is part of the resolution of the issue. Then follow up with the person later but don't be intrusive.

Remember that Jesus said, "You are the salt of the earth" (Matthew 5:12). We are to positively influence others, most of all to lead them to know

211

Christ as their Savior. If the person you meet appears to be having a good day, you can add to it by your smile and hello that affirms interest. Just that positive exchange might help the person to continue with resolving a small or a big issue. The bottom line is that if we can be positive, smiling, affirming, loving and willing to help another person, we are helping to make this a better world for that individual. In the process, we are making our own world a more positive and pleasant one in which to live. How will you greet the next person you meet?

STUDY QUESTIONS

1. How do you typically greet other people you come across at work, church or other places? Could this be improved upon?
2. Think about a time when you met a person who shared some issues in their life with you. What did you do? How did it work out?
3. To show love and concern for others, we can't be too wrapped up in ourselves. We must be other-person centered in order to genuinely portray love and concern for others. Are you other-person centered?

336

"Love is patient, love is kind. It does not envy, it does not boast, it is not proud. It is not rude. It is not self-seeking, it is not easily angered, it keeps no record of wrongs. Love does not delight in evil but rejoices with the truth. It always protects, always trusts, always hopes, always perseveres" I Corinthians 13:4-7

CHANGE IS A NEUTRAL WORD

In recent presidential elections, the candidates tried to outdo each other by promising the greatest amount of change. Change can be very positive when it is needed to bring about positive differences. Change, however, can be very detrimental when the intended or accidental changes are negative.

We are undergoing considerable change in our culture with many people concluding that much of the change is not positive. In what areas, you might ask? The status of marriage, the decline in our ability to produce American goods and services without incurring massive national debt, the statement of political leaders that we are no longer a Christian nation, the decline of many American cities facing decay from within, unemployment due to dominance of foreign goods in our stores and our lack of leadership to recognize our problems and present solutions for their resolution. These are a few areas of change but you could add to the list.

There are many instances of change recorded in the Bible. As Moses was preparing for Joshua to take over the leadership of Israel and lead them into the promised land, Moses no doubt had concerns about all the change they would encounter as they faced their enemies and capturing the promised land. The Lord said to Moses, as recorded in Deuteronomy 31:6: "Do not be afraid or terrified because of them, for the Lord your God goes with you; he will never leave you nor forsake you." With the Lord's help in our lives, we can deal with change in the appropriate ways.

Germany faced severe problems during the 1920s. Their defeat under the Kaiser in World War I and their faltering attempt at democracy led to decline of the currency and national morale. In the early 1930s a man rose to leadership promising change and most Germans were ready for major change. The man was Adolf Hitler and his dynamic change encouraged Germans to believe they were the superior race and that Jews and Christians were the enemy. All of this led Germany to instigate World War II which cost the lives of many Allied Forces, Americans and Germans prior to the defeat of Germany. Change in Germany was not positive.

The next time someone suggests change, ask about the intent of the change, what values they are based on and what the intended effect would be. Change is a neutral word which can lead to either positive good or negative destruction. Before you advocate change, learn more about what effect it will have. Resist negative change while supporting or advocating positive change.

STUDY QUESTIONS

1. Think of at least one change advocated by a public figure that is not likely to bring any improvement to your world. Describe it.
2. The next time you advocate change, describe how it will improve the situation.
3. The opposite of advocating change is to resist change. Think of an instance in which change was resisted when you feel change was needed. 53

While everyone must ensure health, food, and security, people who are wrapped up in themselves see the rest of the world as their servants who are indebted to them and, as a result, might miss the joy of mutual friendship as well as the joy of Christian love, God's grace and salvation.

"The secret of change is to focus all of your energy not on fighting the old, but on building the new." Socrates

Not all change is beneficial. Seek change that will fulfill God's will for man.

COMMUNICATING WITH OTHERS

This week let's talk about how we see ourselves has an impact on our ability to communicate with others. The more insecure we are, the more self-centered we become. The more self-centered we are, the more difficult it is to reach out to others to help them solve their problems or even to understand the nature of their problems.

Author Dr. J. Grant Howard explains that as self-centered persons we tend to "hide or hurl" in our relationships with others. By hurl he means throwing or hurling a negative thought at others. As others are degraded in our mind by the hurling, we think we will feel better about ourselves. However, the process is likely to get us into a downward spiral in which we do more hurling and hiding resulting in further damaging our personal self concept and making it more difficult to reach out to others.

How do we reverse that spiral? There are several steps to be taken. We must begin to think positive thoughts about the person God created when he created us. All people are initially worthy of respect. But we must respect ourselves before others will respect us. Once we begin to see value in our own being, we can then begin to reach out to others. We heal ourselves when we seek to heal others.

When we attempt to communicate with others we have to send more than words. We must effectively communicate a thought (or information), something that the receiving person understands. Whether the communication is successful depends on there being a clear thought in our head, choosing the right words to effectively communicate that thought and a willing listener who is capable of understanding the thoughts being communicated. Don't allow self-doubt to diminish the thought you are communicating or diminish how effectively you communicate it. Speak with confidence and clarity if you expect others to listen. Finally, we must follow the exhortation of Colossians 4:6: "Let your conversation be always full of grace, seasoned with salt, so that you may know how to answer everyone."

STUDY QUESTIONS

1. Do you tend to "hide or hurl" as Dr. Grant describes human behavior?
2. If you are in a downward spiral, how do you plan to reverse it?
3. How do you ensure that what you are communicating is heard and understood by others?

96

"They asked each other, 'Were not our hearts burning within us while He talked with us on the road and opened the Scriptures to us?'" Luke 24:32

"When Jesus therefore saw His mother, and the disciple whom He loved standing by, He said to His mother, 'Woman, behold your son!' Then He said to the disciple, 'Behold your mother!' And from that hour that disciple took her to his own home" John 10:25-26

TEACHING OTHERS

Aristotle once said, "The proof that you know something is that you are able to teach it." Another version of this is, "If you really understand something, you will be able to explain it to others so that they understand it."

When we listen to someone else speak, we don't have to prepare for it. In fact, most people don't even take notes on a talk, lecture or sermon they hear. When we are listeners only and not contributors, we don't sense the need to prepare for the event or even make any record of the event. We look upon speaking by others as our entertainment and we can accept or reject anything we hear.

A true dialog is the next step in involvement. In this case, we are expected or at least given the opportunity to enter into the discussion by questioning, responding, agreeing or disagreeing with what has been said. This might occur in a Sunday School class, in a course in which we are enrolled, in a barber or beauty shop or over a cup of coffee.

However, when we are teaching we take on a higher level of responsibility. James 3:1 tells us, "Not many of you should become teachers, my fellow believers, because you know that we who teach will be judged more strictly." As a teacher we have greater responsibility. This responsibility implies an understanding of the topic or set of topics for one or more sessions. Teaching also implies that the teacher has some expertise in the topics being taught. Teaching implies preparation in advance of the teaching moment. Preparing to teach is in itself a great learning experience. The teacher normally has greater mastery of the subject after the teaching event than anyone for whom the teaching was directed.

All of us do some teaching. Children thrive on being taught. Adults progress through life based on being taught, formally or informally. Much of our influence in society is based on our ability to teach others. Some of our teaching is incidental with people who see our behavior and our words and have the opportunity to copy or reject what they heard or saw. All of us have a much greater impact on others than we realize unless we live alone in a cave. When we do teach we can make this a better world by developing the expertise and preparing for each teaching opportunity. What teaching have <u>you</u> done today?

STUDY QUESTIONS

1. What are your teaching opportunities? How well have you done in meeting these opportunities?
2. Explain what James meant in the Scripture quoted above.
3. Comment on the quote from Aristotle above.

91

"Woe to you, teachers of the law and Pharisees, you hypocrites! You shut the door of the kingdom of Heaven in people's faces. You yourselves do not enter, nor will you let those enter who are trying to" Matthew 23:13

"Show me your ways, Lord, teach me your paths" Psalm 25:4

IF YOU CAN EXPLAIN IT

Albert Einstein is credited with making the statement that if you really understand something you will be able to explain it in the simplest of terms. Have you ever been faced with a complex situation and someone asked you to explain it? Maybe you struggled while attempting to bring all the pieces of it together into an explanation that the person asking the question would understand. Maybe you explained it in technical terms that some people would understand but most of us would still be scratching our heads trying to figure out what you said.

Think about five concepts or projects that are important to either your personal life or are a part of your work life. Try to explain each of them in no more than three written sentences. It might take you some time to carefully select the words you use but that is essential to being articulate. Avoid using comparisons to say "it is just like x y or z" (something that others might recognize). This comparison might be helpful in creating understanding but it still avoids the basic question. Can you explain the concept or project, however complicated it might be, succinctly and clearly so that most people would understand it.

Einstein was a genius at being able to reduce complexity to simplicity. It was because he understood what he was talking about so well that he could explain it simply.

If you didn't succeed at taking five projects or concepts and being able to explain each of them in three sentences or less, this suggests that you need to learn more about the project or concept so that you can get to the three sentence level. Remember that these are not run on sentences that look more like a paragraph. The choice of words in the sentences needs some attention as well so that we don't confuse the recipient with words they do not know or comprehend.

President Calvin Coolidge was known as a man of few words. He was often quoted because he could state his thoughts so succinctly. Try doing this yourself and see if people are more likely to understand what **you** are saying. Look at the many statements by Jesus in the New Testament and notice how brief and to the point they were. Even the parables were no longer than needed to make the illustration clear to the listener.

When a thought is clear in our head, we should be able to explain it to others in words that can be understood by others. If it is not clear to us, we will not be able to explain it to others. When not clear to us, further thinking on our part will be required. It is natural that we will have ideas in our head that we have not yet thought all the way to conclusion so thoughts in development will be fuzzy if we try to explain it prematurely. But a well-developed thought has the capacity to not only change us but also to change the world around us. In developing our thoughts we turn to wisdom but wisdom might take time to surface on a particular idea. Proverbs 16:16 helps us here: "How much better is it to get wisdom than gold, and to get understanding rather than silver" (KJV). We want people to understand what we have to say. Take the time to draw on wisdom and well developed thinking to bring about a world more pleasing to God.

STUDY QUESTIONS

1. Do you tend to be a person of many words or few words? Can you choose the balance between talking most of the time and saying very little to clearly express the thoughts that are within you?
2. How accomplished are you at taking complex subjects and explaining them in terms understandable to most people?
3. Do what is suggested at the beginning of the second paragraph.

110

"We have much to say about this, but it is hard to make it clear to you because you no longer try to understand. In fact, though by this time you ought to be teachers, you need someone to teach you the elementary truths of God's word all over again. You need milk, not solid food!" Hebrews 5:11-12

"With many similar parables, Jesus spoke the word to them, as much as they could understand. He did say not anything to them without using a parable. But when He was alone with His own disciples, he explained everything" Mark 433-34

GIVING THANKS

You might have heard a sermon on giving thanks and you had the opportunity for a Thanksgiving dinner. But did you really give thanks to God and to others who contribute to your life? Truly giving thanks is an act of the mind and not just of the body. Sitting reverently while someone prays is an opportunity for the mind to engage in giving our own thanks but it could be a time when the mind wanders to fixing a meal, how you feel about what someone said or did or your own aches and pains. So if your mind did not get to the point of really giving thanks to God and those who impact your life, NOW would be a good time for giving thanks.

Giving thanks is an attitude of the mind. It is an act of love. See 1 John 3:1 where it reads, "How great is the love the Father has lavished on us, that we should be called the children of God." (NIV-MIT) That we could be called "the children of God" is something for which we should be thankful. Love has been extended to us. But how great is our love toward those around us? Is that love evident every day?

Giving thanks is an act of giving. Giving means something leaves us and goes to God or another person or both. Giving thanks, however, never depletes us but instead enriches us. The more we love, the more we are thankful, the more pleasing we are in the sight of God. So why wouldn't we be loving and thankful every moment of our lives? Satan hates love and being thankful. Satan appeals to our selfish desires. It is up to us to overcome Satan. King David stated well what our guide should be in 1 Chronicles 16:34: "Give thanks to the Lord, for he is good, his love endures forever." If we love we will want to give thanks. Paul, in 1 Corinthians 15:57, tells us "But thanks be to God! He gives us the victory through our Lord Jesus Christ." And thanks be to those around who enrich our lives daily and also to those we do not see as often, those who serve us in our armed forces, in our police and fire departments and in a myriad of other ways that make our lives healthy, safe, productive and enjoyable.

STUDY QUESTIONS

1. Above we stated, "NOW would be a good time for giving thanks." What action does that prompt you to do?

2. Think about the relationship between love (of God and others) and being thankful. Write out a couple of thoughts that come to mind.

3. Think of five people outside of your family for whom you are thankful. Make it a point to say thank you to them in the next seven days.

267

"Let us come before Him with thanksgiving and extol Him with music and song" Psalm 95:2

"Thanks be to God for His indescribable gift" 2 Corinthians 9:15

"Enter the gates with Thanksgiving and His courts with praise; give thanks to Him and praise His name" Psalm 100:4

PRINCIPLES, POWER OR POSITION

Men and women in positions of authority have historically sought these positions in government and other organizations for at least one of three principal reasons: 1) for principle (seeking to ensure principles are followed or results are achieved), 2) power (either for the lust of power or to keep others from exercising it) or 3) position (seeking placement in a position for the benefits of income, security and/or prestige). To be sure, all three might be involved for many people. Then the issue is, how do they rank in importance?

Those who have sought positions of authority because of a commitment to principle or seeking certain results for the greater good could arguably include the first six Presidents of the United States (George Washington, John Adams, Thomas Jefferson, James Madison, James Monroe and John Quincy Adams). They were all guided by a vision of what would be best for the United States. A person seeking authority primarily for principle is a person who sees the greatest advantage of the position being the opportunity to cause the right principles to be put into place or causing certain results for the greater good. George Washington only reluctantly took the position of President because he correctly perceived that his refusal to do so would put the new nation at risk. Non-profit organizations are often led by a person whose motivation is primarily category one, seeking principle or the greater good.

The second category of seeking positions of authority is for the primary reason of seeking personal (and often party) power which could possibly lead to the abuse of power. This means that the use of authority will be guided by how that authority will protect and enhance personal power. Few, if any, of our U S Presidents have sought office for personal power alone although many were seen as persons not guided by many principles. Adolf Hitler would be an example of this type of person seeking authority in order to exercise personal power. The temptation of persons motivated this way is to try to shortcut the process through unethical or criminal action. Hitler did both.

Many people are motivated by the third category, the security of a position and income. There is a position to fill and they have qualified for the position and seek to do what is necessary to retain the position. Yet they are not highly motivated by principle or results for the greater good or even power except to have enough to retain the position and income. In for-profit organizations and for many public office holders the third category can be the primary driving force although there might be some semblance of the first two categories. The organizational culture in many organizations makes it difficult to be motivated by the first category while encouraging the acquisition of power and security.

Jesus sought to have influence over people (to bring them to God) but did so without any position of authority. In fact, those in authority were the ones who resisted him and in time put Him on the cross. Today we are able to have influence without a position of authority through various forms (preaching and teaching, for example). Television personalities offer their opinions, sometimes masked by how they present the news to us. This influence can be either positive or negative depending on the motive of the originator.

Most people have at least some semblance of all three reasons for seeking authority including those motivated primarily by the first category, seeking to work by principle. How does all of this fit God's plan for your service? Each of us should seek to fulfill our understanding of God's plan for us. If that includes positions of authority we should assume such roles as the opportunity presents itself. If we seek God's will, we are likely to be driven by the desire to exercise authority that is largely principle driven and in keeping with God's Word.

STUDY QUESTIONS

1. Which of the three categories best explains your interest in your position?
2. Explain how a person could be motivated by all three?
3. What is the relationship between guided by principle and being guided by God's will for our lives?

POLITICAL OR SOCIAL CORRECTNESS

Read this program in connection with the one that follows in which we address being <u>God</u> correct. At one time political and social correctness was very similar in North America to God correctness. We learned what was socially correct in home, school and church. Being politically correct had to conform to a Christian standard as our leaders attended church and claimed to be Christians. In the most recent presidential elections in the USA, however, neither candidate showed evidence of a Christian faith. We are moving toward basing what is correct, politically and socially, on the individual rather than God. The desire in our society for diversity means a broader acceptance of what is good and acceptable. While this could mean that we are more accepting of one another, we will explore when that is good in next program.

Paul Johnson writes a column in Forbes magazine where he commented: "The mental infection known as 'political correctness' is one of the most dangerous intellectual afflictions ever to attack mankind." Psychologists call this "group think" in which a norm is presented to which everyone is pressured to accept. We learn what is socially and politically correct from TV news and TV programs (crime and comedy). TV has a very subtle impact – what it presents as normal we are expected to believe is correct politically and socially. Powerful groups and lobbyists put enormous pressure on politicians to agree with them. A law passed in North Carolina caused organizations and businesses outside of North Carolina to put considerable social and economic pressure on that State to change the law enacted by their elected representatives to fit the version of political and social correctness held by the outside groups.

Much of what is politically and socially correct has not changed much. It is still socially correct to be considerate to other people. It is still politically correct to talk in positive terms about the U S Constitution. Much of social and political correctness still conforms to the teaching of the Bible. The value of political and social correctness is that it sets standards of acceptable behavior. As Christians we must guard against correctness that runs counter to the Bible.

Some changes in what is socially and politically correct have changed our society for the better. For example, blatant and open discrimination against racial minorities, women and Catholics is no longer publicly tolerated even though not all such discrimination is gone privately.

The USA is still a great country and getting even better in some ways. We need to achieve a balance between individual freedoms to express our views including our religious beliefs and society's social correctness. Standards must exist for stability. In fact, without stability, which comes from standards (what is socially correct), there can be no freedoms. We would live in a state of anarchy. So the key is to find a level of correctness that enhances rather than limits individual freedoms including our freedom to believe in God and live as God would have us live. Christians hold to the standard in John 14:6: "I am the way and the truth and the life." The challenge to Christians is to guard against political and social correctness that is counter to Christian faith thus limiting our freedom of religion.

STUDY QUESTIONS

1. Are there elements of political or social correctness in our society that make you as a Christian uncomfortable? Describe them.
2. What elements of social correctness are you happy to have in place?
3. What do you think is the single greatest threat to our society in what some consider being politically or socially correct?

292

BEING GOD CORRECT

The last program was about political and social correctness. This program will follow up by talking about <u>God</u> correctness. Each of us is influenced in our decisions about what we will do by others. Social correctness guides our efforts as we interact with others. It was pointed out in the previous program that while we need social correctness pressures on us in general to set the norms of acceptable behavior, social and political correctness could go too far in limiting good choices that we can make on things that we stand for. One of the issues in our society today is how social and political correctness might run counter to our Christian faith as more social and political correctness is set by people who do not profess God as well as Jesus as their savior.

The Bible is the guide for Christians as to what is socially correct. Earlier in our history the Bible guided most of society but today Presidents and the United States Supreme Court are making decisions that run counter to the Bible. Television and other media augment this in subtle ways to promote a lifestyle that includes behavior that the Bible condemns. Many Christians accept this gradual deterioration of the Christian lifestyle without really noticing that it is happening. In Canada, we are told; "it is now a crime to talk publicly about what the Bible says about homosexuals." In the United States there is considerable pressure to conform to this changing lifestyle which is based on the assumption that God does not exist.

The Bible is not specific in its guide on all behavior on all issues but it does provide general guidelines as in the Ten Commandments. Social correctness should be based on the Bible and only then expand into the specific aspects of our society. The Bible does not mention traffic lights but their use is essential and in concert with the Bible. We are a democracy in which all people should be able to speak and act in a responsible way within our laws and not feel bullied because of what we are pressured to believe is politically and socially correct.

In the myriad of choices that we Christians must make every day, it would be important to follow the guidelines that the Apostle Paul laid out in his letter to the Philippians in 4:8: "Finally, brothers, whatever is true, whatever is noble, whatever is right, whatever is pure, whatever is lovely, whatever is admirable - if anything is excellent or praiseworthy - think about such things."

When should we resist those who pressure us to be politically and socially correct? 1. When our values and experience tells us that the "correct" proponents do not have the best interests of our country in mind. 2. When political and social correctness violates one or more of the principles found in the Bible. The Bible tells about God correctness. As Christians, the Bible is our primary guide. When political or social correctness disagrees with God correctness, are you willing to speak up?

STUDY QUESTIONS

1. What are some of the <u>influences</u> you experience that urge you to accept as correct what the Bible tells you is not God correct?
2. What <u>issue</u> concerns you the most in our society today?
3. What can you/will you do to stand up for God correctness?

293

"The lamp of the body is the eye. Therefore, when your eye is good, your whole body also is full of light. But when your eye is bad, your body also is full of darkness" Luke 11:34

"But God demonstrates His own love for us, in that while we were still sinners, Christ died for us" Romans 5:8

IS THE WORLD A BETTER PLACE?

Is the world a better place as a result of your being in it? What about your city, your place of work, your church and your home? This is what God expects of you. In Ephesians 1:4, Paul writes, "For he chose us in him before the creation of the world to be holy and blameless in His sight . . ." I John 4:21 tells us that "...Anyone who loves God, must also love their brother and sister."

Now when we love someone, we will do whatever that person asks of us if it is possible and in that person's best interests. Thus, if we <u>do</u> love God, we will want to make this world a better place than the way we found it by demonstrating love for this person and others needing our assistance.

How can we make this world a better place?

One way is that we can love God and our brothers and sisters. When we do this, our love extends to all people and things we encounter. As we model love, others can see how to follow our footsteps. Love can lead us to "make someone else's day" through a compliment, a word of encouragement or just listening.

Second, we can take care of our health and our standing in the community so that we can be better servants of God. Taking care of ourselves includes having a positive attitude toward others and the world in which we live.

Third, look for opportunities to volunteer either on a regular basis or as needed. There are people and organizations where your help can make a difference.

Fourth, we can exercise care of God's creation. The earth provides resources for our lives and it provides beauty for our enjoyment. We should be careful to utilize this for today and future generations.

Lastly, we can be a person of faith, integrity, cheerfulness, helpfulness and a dutiful worker. We can provide hope, love and encouragement to others. Which of these actions and characteristics will you evident in you today?

STUDY QUESTIONS

1. What can you do this week to further implement the first suggestion above?
2. When was the last time you volunteered to help a person or an organization toward making this a better place? Did you also enjoy doing it?
3. What about your care of God's earth? Are you careful in the use of the resources and appreciative of the beauty God created?

2A

"Therefore, I urge you, brothers and sisters, in view of God's mercy, to offer your bodies as a living sacrifice, holy and pleasing to God – this your true and proper worship" Romans 12:1

"I have told you these things, so that in me you may have peace. In this world you will have trouble. But take heart! I have overcome the world" John 16:33

"Therefore I exhort first of all that supplications, prayers, intercessions, and giving of thanks be made for all men, for kings and all who in authority, that we may lead a quiet and peaceable life in all godliness and reverence" 1 Timothy 2:1-2

"Then the chief priests and Pharisees gathered a council and said, 'What shall we do? For this Man works many signs'" John 11:47

"'But I want you to know that the Son of Man has authority on earth to forgive sins.' So He said to the paralyzed man, 'Get up, take your mat and go home'" Matthew 9:6

"You suffered along with those in prison and joyfully accepted the confiscation of your property, because you knew that you yourselves had better and lasting possessions" Hebrews 10:34

IT'S NOT ALL ABOUT ME

Each of us needs to make a distinction between what we need and what we want. We have needs for food, clothing, shelter and human relationships. There are many things we WANT beyond this but we should set our prioritized goals and use our time with a primary emphasis on needs. What are these basic needs? In 1 Timothy 6:7 the believers were told to "...put their hope in God, who richly provides us with everything for our enjoyment." We need to talk to God, eat something and drink something every day, stay out of the rain and the cold, take care of our health, meet our obligations, relate effectively with those around us and take a shower or bath once in a while. Once we are in the process of meeting these basic needs, we should devote the rest of our time and energies to three priorities:

Number one priority is to worship and serve God. Serving God includes serving others as well as being in a worshipful attitude and taking at least some time each week in which we gather with others to more formally worship God. That sounds a lot like going to Church every Sunday.

Number two priority is to identify the needs of others and serve them. However needy you might consider yourself to be, there is someone nearby who has even greater needs. In time of sorrow or other great need, it is tempting to think only of self. While a grieving period is needed, one of the best ways out of it is to return to focusing on how you will help others meet their needs. Doing so will not only divert attention away from our problems but will also be part of our joy in life that will help us to regain our balance in how we see ourselves. If God has blessed us with ample material benefits, this gives us a chance to share these blessings by enriching the lives of others.

Third, if we have concentrated on the two priorities just mentioned, it is fine to focus on our wants that time, money and energy permit without harming either of the first two priorities. Meeting our wants can bring happiness to us and indirectly to others who see a person who is enjoying life. Our wants need to be limited by what is in keeping with God's will, what is ethical and what makes sense as well as fits our available time, money and energy.

Note that basic needs and all three priorities can be going on at the same time by a careful blending of time, money and energy. "It's A Wonderful Life" but to enjoy it we need to distinguish between needs and wants and focus in succeeding order on the three priorities mentioned. It's a balancing act but we can do it.

STUDY QUESTIONS

1. How would you define your NEEDS? (See the tentative list above)
2. What is your plan for meeting priority number one?
3. What are your WANTS in life? To what extent are they already met? What is next on the list?

157

"To fear the Lord is to hate evil. I hate pride and arrogance, evil behavior and perverse speech" Proverbs 8:13

"For where you have envy and selfish ambition, there you find disorder and every evil practice" James 3:16

"And there came a voice out of the cloud, saying, 'This is my beloved Son: hear Him.'" Luke 9:35

"When the righteous are in authority, the people rejoice; but when the wicked beareth rule, the people mourn." Proverbs 29:2 KJV

IF PEOPLE LIKE YOU

Think about how people react to you and this principle: If people like you, they will find a way to praise you. If they don't like you, they will find a way to criticize you.

To follow this principle, it is clear that you will want to find a way for people to like you. What would cause people to like you? A key to causing people to like us is for <u>us</u> to like other people. If you don't like most people you meet, don't expect them to like you. Your attitude toward others will be apparent regardless of any attempt to conceal your feelings. Second, you must like yourself. When you like yourself, you will be more joyful, pleasant and smiling. When you are confident in yourself, you will find it easier to then find the good in others. When you find the good in others, you bring out the best in them and thus encouraging them in turn to find good in others, including you.

A third way to cause others to like you is to show an interest in what matters to them. Ask questions about what motivates them, what they like to do, what they have accomplished and show an interest in their responses with follow-on questions. People in general enjoy talking about what is important to them. Seek those things out and encourage them to talk (or write) about these topics.

A fourth way is to give genuine positive feedback. Rather than waiting for them to take a breath so that you can talk about yourself, find ways to praise them for their accomplishments, thank them for their service, identify with what is important to them. Avoid negativity. Don't criticize other people, places or things. By being positive, you encourage others to be positive.

Now all of this must be 100% genuine. Others will see through a fake interest and will put you in a worse situation than if you had said nothing at all.

Going back to the principle stated at the beginning, if people like you, they will find a way to praise you. If they <u>don't</u> like you, they will find a way to criticize you. There are complicating factors such as how people feel about others around you, a product or service you represent and how they feel about themselves. However, the principle says, if they like you they will find a way to praise you. That is to say, if they like you, they might find a way to overlook other factors that they find less pleasant.

People are more likely to respond positively to an individual than to a product or a service. Set out to find ways for people to like you rather than thinking that what you represent will simply sell itself regardless of how they respond to you. What you represent is likely to be rejected if the person does not like you.

What changes in your thinking, in your attitude toward people, work and the rest of the world are necessary to make this work for you? Do you wake up thinking of the many opportunities you have today to do good things, to enjoy life and to please God? If you can wake up this way and maintain that attitude during the day, you might discover some new friends and new sources of happiness. Think first of God, then others and then self. Jesus gave us this command: "Do to others as you would have do to you" (Luke 6:31). Be a joyful spirit as you relate to others. What are **you** doing today to cause people to like you?

STUDY QUESTIONS

1. Identify five characteristics you possess that could cause people to like you.
2. To what extent are these five characteristics apparent to everyone you meet?
3. Are there things about you that get negative reactions? Are they important enough to you to continue them as they are or could there be room for change?

102B

"Do not seek revenge or bear a grudge against anyone among your people, but love your neighbor as yourself. I am the Lord" Leviticus 19:18

"Therefore, humble yourselves under the mighty hand of God, that He may exalt you in due time" 1 Peter 4:6

"But if we walk in the light as He is in the light, we have fellowship with one another, and the blood of Jesus His Son cleanses us from all sin" 1 John 1:7

"Listen, I tell you a mystery. We will not all sleep, but we will all be changed – in a flash, in the twinkling of an eye, at the last trumpet. For the trumpet will sound, the dead will be raised imperishable, and we will be changed. For the perishable must clothe itself with imperishable, and the mortal with immortality. When the perishable has been clothed with imperishable, and the mortal with immortality, then the saying that is written will come true. 'Death has been swallowed up in victory.'" 1 Corinthians 15:51-54

CHAPTER SIX

FAITH AND OUR RELATIONSHIP TO GOD

Joy of Being a Christian, Untested Faith, Unforgiving Spirit, Doctrine Driven Life, This Little Light of Mine, Christian Worldview, Ego and Salvation, Keeping His Commands, Earnest Prayer, City on a Hill, The Greatest Gift, Faith and Confidence, Amazing Grace

YOUR FAVORITE WORD

John 3:16 in the Holy Bible is a powerful statement. Have you ever thought about what your favorite word is in this statement? Max Lucado said his favorite word is "Whoever" which talks about the fact that salvation is offered to everyone if only they will believe. The wording of John 3:16 in the NIV is "For God so loved the world that he gave his one and only son, that whoever believes in Him shall not perish, but have eternal life."

Let's look at some of the other words that might be your favorite.

1. God – God is the subject in the sentence. It is about His action, His willingness to reach out to people in offering salvation.
2. Loved – A powerful action word indicating God's attitude toward us. He loves us. What could be more important than that? John 3:16 says God "so loved" telling us that God's love was abundant.
3. World - God's love extends throughout the world to people of all nations, all languages, all colors and all cultures. It is all inclusive.
4. Gave - It doesn't say sold or bargained. It is offered to anyone willing to accept it. What greater gift could there be?
5. One and only Son – If you are a parent, think of your child and giving up that child to be sacrificed. If you are a son or daughter,

think of being sacrificed to benefit the world. What greater sacrifice could there be?

6. Whoever – God extends His love to everyone regardless of what they have done or not done in life. It is not something we can earn, we are just to accept.

7. Believes in Him – This is all we have to do to spend eternity in Heaven. We don't have to be a biblical scholar; we don't even have to understand every concept in the Bible.

8. Shall not perish – We are told we will not go to Hell which is described in the Bible.

9. Have eternal life – Eternal life in Heaven with God. What a gift to receive, to know, to have the assurance of life everlasting in Heaven.

God offers a gift that only requires that we believe in Him. No other conditions. How could we turn down a deal like that? What is YOUR favorite word in John 3:16 or in some other part of the Bible?

STUDY QUESTIONS

1. What is your favorite word in John 3:16?
2. What is John describing as God's gift to us?
3. Why don't more people accept this gift?

120

"Christ is the climax of the Old Testament expectations and the foundation for New Testament Christianity." Dr. D. A. Carson, Trinity Evangelical Divinity School

"I am the way and the truth and the life. No one comes to the Father except through me. If you really know me, you would know my Father as well. From now on, you do know Him and have seen Him." John 14:6-7

A DOCTRINE DRIVEN LIFE

What does it means to have A DOCTRINE DRIVEN LIFE. Doctrine is what the Bible teaches us. Our behavior should follow the doctrine provided to us. Much has been written and said in recent years in Christian circles about the desirability of having a purpose driven life. We accomplish much from having clear purposes in our life. However, while the evangelist Billy Graham has led a purpose driven life, the gangster Al Capone also had a purpose driven life. The difference between the two was what the purposes were based upon. Al Capone's values included making a profit from illegal operations that negatively affected many other people. He cared little about others as long as he acquired what he wanted in life (his purposes).

In contrast, look at the life of the evangelist Billy Graham. Recently deceased, we can look back at a life that was certainly purpose driven with those purposes based on sound Christian doctrine. Mr. Graham had a focus, a purpose, that has centered on the doctrine of salvation - bringing people to Jesus Christ thus allowing them to spend eternity in Heaven. It is significant that Billy Graham had these purposes that were based on Christian doctrine found in the Bible.

Christian faith is based on how we understand and act on the basic tenets of the faith, Christian doctrine. Christian doctrine includes our concept of God, Jesus Christ, the Bible, the nature and mission of the Church, faith, repentance, baptism, the Lord's Supper, prayer, giving, the resurrection, the second coming, Christian love, sin, Satan, Heaven, hell, the two Covenants, pardon, person and gift of the Holy Spirit, holiness, spiritual gifts and worship. There are other tenets as well, significant for a group of believers to base a church on one or more doctrines. Our Christian faith comes from our understanding of these doctrines. Where do you stand on each of these doctrines? What you do in Church on Sunday, and the way in which you show your Christian faith during the week, is a reflection of your understanding of these doctrines.

Our understanding of these doctrines is central to our personal value system. What a person values, what he or she believes in, is the essence of his or her faith that in turn determines behavior and purposes in life. Purposes could be good or evil. If they are purposes that honor the doctrines relating to God, they are good purposes. If they honor Satan, they are not good purposes. If Al Capone had not had a purpose driven life, society would have been better off. Paul encouraged the young preacher, Titus, to seek leaders for the church who would "hold firmly to the trustworthy message as it has been taught, so that he can encourage others by sound doctrine and refute those who would oppose it." Look at your purposes in life, are they based on the whims of the day, on what others tell you should be your purpose, your personal desires, or are they based on solid Christian doctrine?

STUDY QUESTIONS

1. Which elements of Christian doctrine are the driving forces in your life?
2. Are your purposes in life consistent with the Christian doctrines that form your Christian faith?
3. Look at the list of Christian doctrines above. Is there one or more that trouble you to the extent that you are uncertain of where you stand on that particular doctrine? What are going to do about it?

320A

"It is for freedom that Christ set us free. Stand firm, then, and do not let yourselves be burdened by a yoke of slavery" (sin) Galatians 5:1

A CHRISTIAN WORLDVIEW

Having a Christian worldview means that our thinking and perception of the world is based on our Christian faith and that whatever we think, say and do is from that perspective. Dr. Edward M. Curtis at Biola University (*Transformed Thinking*, JKO Publishing, 1996) tells that a Christian worldview is "transformed." Dr. Curtis calls it "thinking Christianly." It is easy for all of us to respond to issues and questions from our preset bias and usual responses without engaging the mind to search for answers from a clear Christian worldview. Dr. Curtis adds: "I am worried by the ideas, sometimes found in the church, that seriously using the mind and developing the intellect will get us into trouble and that true spirituality involves a kind of uncritical, unthinking mysticism where God simply directs us at every turn."

Dr. Curtis refers us to Romans 12:2 which reads: "Do not conform to the pattern of this world, but be transformed by the renewing of your mind. Then you will be able to test and approve what God's will is – his good, pleasing and perfect will." Think about what "the renewing of your mind" means to you right now. Romans 12:2 is telling us this "renewing" is a prerequisite to serving God's will.

Everyone has a worldview as Dr. David S. Dockery reminds us (*Renewing Minds*, 2007). You might remember Archie Bunker. He had a worldview. He could tell you his thoughts on any topic. Each of <u>us</u> has a worldview. The issue is: on what is that worldview based? Archie or Jesus? Jesus introduced us to the Christian worldview. As we work toward being more Christ like, we begin to understand a Christian worldview and how much we need to think from that perspective. Dr. Dockery helps us understand the concept: "An examined and thoughtful worldview, however, is more than a private, personal viewpoint; it is a comprehensive life system that seeks to answer the basic questions of life. A Christian worldview is not just one's personal faith expression, nor is it simply a theory. It is an all-consuming way of life, applicable to all spheres of life."

Both Dr. Dockery and Dr. Curtis remind us that integration of faith with all other aspects of life and a clear understanding of reality are essential.

Each of us has societal values cast at us every day and so many of them sound reasonable because of their similarity in some ways to the values we already hold. The values presented by television are far from a Christian worldview but they are hammered at us every day until we might accept them as the norm and think they are consistent with a Christian worldview. In Ephesians 4:23 Paul urges us "to be made new in the attitude of our minds." We are told to think for ourselves and not just be another copy of what is socially correct. We must "think Christianly" constantly to be the person God intends for us to be.

How do we "think Christianly" constantly? We must be in touch with the reality around us but not let society determine how we should think. Dr. Curtis reminds us "the human mind is a wonderful gift from God." Let us utilize that mind to read our Bibles, remain in prayer continually, associate with other Christians and conclude that we <u>will</u> have a Christian worldview. By doing so, we please God and work with God to serve mankind.

STUDY QUESTIONS

1. Do you "think Christianly?" What evidence can you provide to show to God that this is true?
2. What is your most significant block to having a Christian worldview? Is it people you associate with, television, what you read, where you work, where you shop?
3. "Renewing your mind" is not a simple task. Paul tells all of us that we need to do this and not just once in life. Where should you start?

390A

"Jesus looked at them and said, 'With man this is impossible, but not with God; all things are possible with God'" Mark 10:27

FAITH, CONFIDENCE AND ACCOMPLISHMENT

Faith in God and confidence in self can be a powerful package to bring about accomplishments in life. Faith in God is offered to us free, all we have to do is accept it and then live it. Confidence in ourselves has no price tag either but both elude many of us. Part of the challenge is how we combine faith in God with self-confidence. Too much self-confidence leaves no room for faith in God while the lack of self-confidence makes faith in God difficult as well. We need to achieve a balanced self perspective that values who and what we are as a child of God which means we put God first, others second and ourselves third. Third is still a very important place.

How do we find faith in God and self-confidence? Faith in God can be found by reading the Bible and with associating with Christians who are clear about their faith in God. Confidence in self can be found by getting a good handle on our capabilities, our talents and our gifts as well as spending time with those who have a good balance of self-confidence and a Christian faith.

The third part of our topic is accomplishment and this comes when we have found that balance between faith in God and self-confidence and then apply goals. To do this, understand the truth of Romans 10:17: … "faith comes from hearing the message, and the message is heard through the word about Christ." The message is the Word of God, the Bible. Christ came to bring forgiveness of sin and a new redeemed life that seeks to live out God's will for our lives. Your faith in God and your confidence can help you accomplish goals that will make a difference in this world.

STUDY QUESTIONS

1. Think about the first sentence above as it applies to you.
2. How would you rate your self-confidence?
3. Is your Christian faith clear enough to explain it to others?

36

"Rejoice in the Lord always." Philippians 4:4

"A heart knoweth its own bitterness; . . ." Proverbs 14:10

"For wisdom is better than rubies; and all the things that might be desired are not to be compared to it." Proverbs 9:11

"You, dear children, are from God and have overcome them, because the one who is in you is greater than the one who is in the world." 1 John 4:4

"My sheep listen to my voice; I know them, and they follow me. I give them eternal life, and they shall never perish; no one can snatch them out of my hand" John 10:27

UNTESTED FAITH

Untested faith is unreliable. When we buy a car or a dishwasher, we know that the product has gone through extensive testing before it was made available for purchase. Companies spend considerable amounts of money on research in order to test products. We might even consult a *Consumers Report* to see what their tests indicate is the best product of that type. .

God created us with the period in our lives in which we are transformed from a baby to a young adult during which time we test ourselves and others test us. By the time we reach adulthood we are still testing ourselves in most aspects of life. As we find our gifts and talents, we are likely to find areas in which we feel the test has been successful. We continue to test ourselves as we mature in our work, in our family relationships and in our Christian faith.

While products we buy are tested, our Christian faith also will be tested. James 1:2 reads: "Consider it pure joy, my brothers and sisters, whenever you face trials of many kinds." Notice that James said "whenever" and not if. We will face trials in life. It is through these trials that our faith either grows deeper or it withers. It withers if we expect the Christian life to be without trials. Jesus talked (Mt 13:23) about the seed that fell on good soil that produced much. We find out if our faith is planted in good soil when we face trials. When we do, we can look to God or look inward to ourselves. When we look to ourselves we think of why me because we lack good soil. We might expect the Christian life to be without trials and to be marked only by God's blessings on us. But when our focus is on God rather than ourselves, our untested faith becomes stronger. Dr. Charles Stanley made the comment that "untested faith is unreliable." James 1:3-4 goes on to say that "the testing of your faith produces perseverance. Let perseverance finish its work so that you might be mature and complete, not lacking anything." We should learn from the testing of our faith. We are tested when we meet opportunities for sin, are able to recognize it as sin and decide to turn away. We fail the test if we don't turn away.

So what is the test of our faith in dealing with temptation? How do we decide that sin is actually sin? How can we tell the difference between sin and blessing? There has to be some standard by which we make that decision. If we have to rely on others to tell us, our faith is shallow. If we can quote the Bible but don't understand what we are quoting, our faith is superficial and not in good soil. Our faith does not require understanding everything in the Bible. Our faith does require that we understand John 3:16 and Acts 2. Our faith requires that we understand salvation and that it is something that we sincerely desire for ourselves. When we are saved, we are tested to see if the roots of our faith are strong enough to persist in the storms of life. How deep is the soil where your Christian faith is planted? When your faith has been tested in the past, how well did you do? How are you doing today with the tests of your faith?

If your faith is being tested right now, do three things: Pray, read Bible passages such as Romans 3:23 and talk with a person whose faith has been proven to be strong to discuss your test. Spend some time in solitary prayer to talk with God, repent of the sin in your life and then leave your burden with Him (Acts 2:38). Cleanse the negative from your mind and stand firm (Ephesians 6:10-17). God's grace will be sufficient (2 Cor 12:9) for a new day in Jesus Christ (Mark 14:25).

STUDY QUESTIONS

1. Are you facing a test of your faith right now? The first step in combating it is to describe it. Write out a brief description of that test.
2. When you faced a test of your faith in the past, was the soil deep enough to allow your Christian faith to persevere, to win out?
3. Are there elements in the culture where you live that provide a constant challenge to your Christian faith? How well are you handling these elements?

302

THIS LITTLE LIGHT OF MINE

This week our topic is THIS LITTLE LIGHT OF MINE. There is a song we might have learned very early in Sunday School. It goes like this:

> This little light of mine
> I'm going to let it shine
> This little light of mine
> I'm going to let it shine, let it shine, let it shire, let it shine.

Other verses start with "Let it shine till Jesus comes" and "Hide it under a bushel, NO" closing with "I'm going to let it shine."

Does your light shine? Are you going to let it shine till Jesus comes or are you going to hide it under a "bushel" to keep others from seeing it. We all have a light to shine and through the use of that light we can work to make this a better world, one in which Christian values and faith are extended to others making their life better both here and helping them on their way to heaven.

But our light must be in balance. Our light should not be designed to keep other lights from shining or to be the only one that is lit. Our light needs to work in concert with other lights. On a Christmas tree there is usually only one light that is much brighter than all of the others and that represents the angel at the top, the representative of God. Our light should be one that encourages other lights.

How do we get our light and other lights to shine? Dwight L. Moody, the evangelist, once said, "We are told to let our light shine, and if it does, we won't have to tell anybody it does. Lighthouses don't fire cannons to call attention to their shining – they just shine."

When we let our light shine, do others know it is a Christian light? Does it illumine our faith and our Christian values? Is that light shining where it is needed with the poor and hungry? Is that light shining with those in some form of distress? Is that light showing love and caring wherever it glows? Does that light encourage others to be Christians? Jesus exhorted His followers to "let your light shine before others, that they may see your good deeds and glorify your Father in heaven" (Matthew 5:16). Our light might be small but it can be mighty in serving God by living an exemplary life through our devotion to God and our passion for serving others. Let's let our little light shine.

STUDY QUESTIONS

1. Is your Christian light shining? How far away can it be seen? Far enough for others to see it?
2. When have you helped someone else to get their light to shine? Has it continued to shine?
3. Is there a possibility that your light could reach more people and have a greater effect? What would it take?

359

"Your word is a lamp for my feet, a light on my path" Psalm 119:105

"Mockers stir up a city, but wise men turn away anger." Proverbs 9:8

"These have come so that the proven genuineness of your faith – of greater worth than gold, which perishes even though refined by fire – may result in praise, glory and honor when Jesus Christ is revealed" 1 Peter 1:7

"For you know that it was not with perishable things such as silver or gold that you were redeemed from the empty way of life handed down to you from your ancestors, but with the precious blood of Christ, a lamb without blemish or defect" 1 Peter 1:18

I'D RATHER HAVE JESUS

Luther Green Presley wrote the words for *I'd Rather Have Jesus* with the music composed later by George Beverly Shea. The song has these words:

> I'd rather have Jesus than silver or gold;
> I'd rather be his than have riches untold.
> I'd rather have Jesus than houses or land.
> Yes I'd rather be led by his nail pierced hands
> Than to be the king of a vast domain and be held in sins dread sway;
> I'd rather have Jesus than anything this world affords today
>
> I'd rather have Jesus than worldly applause;
> I'd rather be faithful to his dear cause.
> I'd rather have Jesus than worldwide things;
> I'd rather be true to his holy name.

Most people spend much of their effort in pursuit of silver or gold, riches untold and houses or land. We buy lottery tickets in order to acquire these things. We move to a better paying job to have these things. We save in order to have these things. But would we rather have Jesus when faced with a choice between the two? If so, would the money for the lottery ticket go into the church collection plate? Would we support missions and special programs at our church? Would we be in church every Sunday instead of once in a while or just Christmas and Easter (C & E Christians as one of my professors used the term)?

The silver and gold, riches untold and houses or land are all left behind when our lives here end or the second coming occurs, whichever one is first. We can have Jesus both on this earth and in the life beyond in Heaven. We can have Jesus AND some silver and gold, riches untold as well as houses or land on this earth. If we would rather have Jesus, then Jesus will be our number one.

We can look at our calendar (appointment book) and our checkbook (credit card statements) to see if we would really rather have Jesus. Much of our time and money must go to maintain our lives (housing, work) but what about the time and money expended beyond what is necessary? Does the amount for the boat payment, the extra car or vacations compare well with what we spend in time and money on our Church and other Christian activities? How well can you say, I'd rather have Jesus than silver or gold? In addition to silver and gold, expenditures of time and talent can be for children and others in need as Jesus commanded (Luke 16:16)

In addition to time, talent (God's gifts) and money, there is our attitude. If we would rather have Jesus than riches untold, then our attitude should reflect the life of Jesus Christ. Kindness, empathy, generosity, listening, helping, caring, loving and fellowship are all characteristics of Jesus that we should emulate if we would rather have Jesus than silver or gold. Matthew 6:33 tells us, "But seek first his kingdom and His righteousness, and all these things (needs & possessions) will be given to you as well." How we live our lives here tells whether we really would rather have Jesus.

STUDY QUESTIONS

1. What evidence can you provide from your life today that you would rather have Jesus than silver or gold?
2. Is there anything in your life today that is contrary evidence that you would rather have Jesus (something Jesus would not do or have)?
3. What changes could you make for the future that would show to God that you really mean it when you say I'd rather have Jesus?

362

AMAZING GRACE

The song Amazing Grace was written in 1772, in Olney, England by John Newton. He had led a rough life including involvement in the slave trade but had an experience on a ship when he called to God to save the ship. This began a turnabout in which he studied for the ministry and was assigned a church in Olney. From here he wrote many songs. Amazing Grace became popular in the United States in the early 19th century and is now the favorite Christian hymn on this side of the Atlantic.

The words of the first verse reflect the tumultuous set of experiences that marked his life prior to writing the song. These words are:

> Amazing grace! How sweet the sound
> That saved a wretch like me!
> I once was lost, but now am found;
> Was blind, but now I see.

Written in the first person, Newton related how his prior life had not been what God wanted ("a wretch like me"). Each of us might look at our life to date and think about how close it comes to being the life that God would have wanted for us. Newton knew God existed – he called to Him in a moment of despair. Do we only call upon God when our life has gone awry?

The second verse goes like this:

> Through many dangers, toils and snares,
> I have already come;
> 'Tis grace hath brought me safe this far,
> And grace will lead me home.

Grace has been said to be unmerited favor. Newton felt he had received the grace of God. Grace had brought him "safe this far." The final verse sings of his next ten thousand years:

When we've been there ten thousand years,
Bright shining as the sun;
We've no less days to sing God's praise
Than when we'd first begun.

In the years when my Mother was alive, she would play the piano and ask me to sing with her. Once when we had sung this verse, she remarked about how ten thousand years from now we could still sing of God's praise.

Grace is amazing when we consider that regardless of whether we have lived a life like John Newton or a more typical life in which sin still abounds, grace is sufficient to give each of us eternal life. Grace allows a blanket forgiveness of our sins (only blasphemy of God is not forgiven). All we have to do is ask God for forgiveness of our sins, whatever they are (1 John 1:9). We ask for forgiveness in the form of prayer. This prayer means we believe in God and we want Him to guide our lives away from sin. But grace extends to more than sin. Grace and God's love are with us in trials and tribulation. Amazing grace is available to everyone if they only believe. Are you allowing God's grace into your life?

STUDY QUESTIONS

1. What is the amazing part of John Newton's life and his relationship to God?
2. What is God's grace? What does it do for us? Who are the recipients?
3. What is amazing about grace? Does it apply to your life?

404

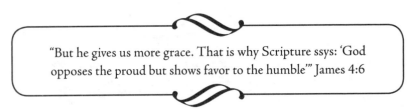

"But he gives us more grace. That is why Scripture ssys: 'God opposes the proud but shows favor to the humble'" James 4:6

CITY ON A HILL

This message is about a CITY ON A HILL. Matthew 5:14 reads, "You are the light of the world. A city built on a hill cannot be hidden." Early colonists called their settlement a "citie on a hill" based on this passage. The concept applies to us individually but also to what we establish as in the colonial village. Jesus told us in the Sermon on the Mount to "...let your light shine before others, that they may see your good deeds, and glorify your Father in Heaven" (Mt 5:16).

John Winthrop used the term "city on a hill" when addressing a group of Puritans who would make up the first group of colonists from the Massachusetts Bay group to go to the new world. In his sermon called "A Model of Christian Charity" in March 1690, he warned them that they would be seen "as a city upon a hill, the eyes of the people are upon us." He went on to say "So that if we shall deal falsely with our God in this work we have undertaken and so cause Him to withdraw this present from us, we shall be made a story and a byword through the world."

When we join a church we become part of a fellowship that is "a city on a hill" because as John Winthrop reminded the Puritans, the community around us sees what the church does and what it stands for. The reputation of a church as a loving congregation that is serious about its faith is created by what the members do in that community. If the light burns dimly the community might not know the church exists but if the light in the church burns brightly, the light will be seen afar because it is on a hill, whether it physically sits on high ground or not. Churches, like people, can go astray by concentrating on works without faith or becoming primarily a social organization that happens to meet on the Sabbath. Each of us has the responsibility of ensuring that our church has a strong faith in God that is clearly shown in the community. Each of us is one, but one person is able to lead and to exemplify the Christian life that Jesus taught.

While we might keep the church's light shining brightly, we are expected even more to keep our own light shining "because the eyes of the people are upon us" as John Winthrop stated it. As we grow older in years and stature, we are seen by more people than we realize. Just as others influence us, others are influenced by what we say and do and even by what we don't do. When we claim to be a Christian, our beacon as a Christian begins to shine. Others decide whether to be a Christian or to attend church in part based on what the Christians they encounter say and do.

The Sermon on the Mount (Matthew 5) was training for the disciples of Jesus in preparation for going forth into the world to spread the word. We are His disciples and need to be familiar with what Jesus said in this Scripture. Our light will not shine brightly if we don't know what the Bible says while learning the fundamentals of the Christian faith. It also will not burn brightly if we "put it under a bowl" (Matthew 5:15). In order for a "city built on a hill" to be seen at some distance, its many lights must be viewed by those who are drawn to it. Is your light sufficiently bright to draw others to your Christian faith?

STUDY QUESTIONS

1. Is the church where you worship a "city on a hill" by letting others know that it exists to draw others to the Christian faith or is it a social club?
2. Read the Sermon on the Mount again in Matthew 5. What is the message that Jesus brings to you in this passage?
3. How brightly is your light shining to proclaim your Christian faith? Do people who see you often know that you are a Christian? If so, how do they know this?

417

"Neither do people light a lamp and put it under a bowl. Instead they put it on its stand, and it gives light to everyone in the house" Matthew 5:15

EARNEST PRAYER

Think about what earnest prayer would be. Jesus was critical of the Pharisees for their prayer which was for show and not earnest. In Samuel 1, we see two prayers of the godly woman named Hannah. She was the wife of Elkanah. Hannah prayed earnestly that she would have a child (1 Samuel 1:10-17). From her prayer we can learn characteristics of earnest prayer. First, Hannah was able to pray earnestly even in her sorrow and bitterness. It is tempting for us to show anger when we are bitter and in sorrow rather than talk with God earnestly.

Second, she prayed from her heart. These were not repetitious words spoken by habit but rather words that reflected what was most important to Hannah at that point in her life.

Third, she asked for something positive that, while it would bring satisfaction to her, was even more significant in what it would do for others. She prayed for a child who she would "give to the Lord" for service on behalf of God. Hannah prayed for a need, not just a want.

Fourth, Hannah prayed with a covenant. She promised that she would turn the son over to God's service for the rest of his life. She meant it and she kept her promise by turning the baby Samuel over once he had been weaned, visiting him when they went to the annual feast.

An interesting part of Hannah's prayer is that it was followed by another prayer in which she thanked God for answering her prayer (1 Samuel 2). How often do we thank God for the blessings that have been sent our way?

Prayer is simply a talk with God in which we ask for forgiveness of our sins, let God know of our needs and ask for God to intervene in events and the lives of others for healing or other individual needs and for forgiveness. God knows our innermost thoughts but prayer is a time when we acknowledge God's role in our lives as well as seek to praise, give thanks, tell Him of our needs and repent.

Prayer in earnest, rather than mindless rituals of meaningless and thoughtless words, is what God wants to hear from us. The next time you pray, make it an earnest prayer.

STUDY QUESTIONS

1. Thinking back on your prayers of the last week, to what extent have they been earnest prayers?
2. What steps do you need to take to make your prayers more earnest?
3. Do your prayers acknowledge God's role in your life as well as seek to praise, give thanks and tell Him of your needs?

152

"The harvest is plentiful but the workers are few. Ask the Lord of the harvest, therefore, to send out workers into his harvest field." Jesus Christ in Matthew 9:37-38

"Peter replied, 'Repent and be baptized, every one of you, in the name of Jesus Christ for the forgiveness of your sins. And you will receive the gift of the Holy Spirit'" Acts 2:38

"Jesus answered and said, 'I am the way and the truth and the life. No one comes to the Father except through me'" John 14:6

BITTERNESS AND FORGIVENESS

We might deal with being upset by being angry. Anger can turn to long-term bitterness if that anger remains. But how do we resolve anger?

You have maybe read about a case in which a person was murdered yet the family of the victim forgave the person who committed the crime and reached out to that person in prayer and forgiveness. That takes a lot of fortitude to overcome the natural inclination to anger for the loss that has been inflicted by a person who did not care about a loved one. Yet that is what forgiveness is all about. Forgiveness is concentrating on the person who committed the act rather than the act itself. We cannot change history. We cannot change or control the facts. What we can control is how we react to what has happened.

Think back to when someone did something or said something that upset you. How did you react? Do you still have some bitterness related to that incident? If so, think of how Jesus dealt with the woman at the well. It was clear that she had sinned but Jesus forgave her. Ephesians 4:31 tells us, "Get rid of all bitterness, rage and anger, brawling and slander, along with every form of malice." Bitterness can control us.

Are you able to forgive every person who has done something or said something that has upset you, has made you angry? When we fail to forgive, we pay the penalty of having to carry that anger around with us wherever we go. If you have not yet forgiven others, pray for forgiveness. You will no longer have to carry that bitterness around with you. You then have the opportunity to be more cheerful and positive in your relationships with others. It will also change your relationship with God when forgiveness has taken place. We cannot be the person God wants us to be when we carry a burden. Release the burden and come closer to God. Those around you will notice that you no longer have this load and can now concentrate on greater service to God and mankind.

STUDY QUESTIONS

1.   Are you still bitter about some incident years ago? Why is that?

2. If so, are you enjoying your anger and bitterness? Who is benefitting from this anger and bitterness?

3. Are you fully engaged in serving God and mankind?

19

"There isn't time, so brief is life, for bickerings, apologies, heartburnings, callings to account. There is only time for loving, and but an instant, so to speak, for that." Mark Twain

"If your Bible is falling apart, it usually means that you are not." Anonymous

"Disciplined, consistent study of God's word and regular participation in a Bible teaching ministry are critical for the growth of our spiritual lives as Christians." Pastor Dr. David Jeremiah

"I am profitably engaged reading the Bible. Take all of this Book upon reason that you can, and the balance on faith, and you will live and die a better man." President Abraham Lincoln

OUR WILL OR OBEDIENCE?

Human beings generally enjoy having things their way. We like to have our will followed by others. In expressing our will, we often confuse opinion with fact. Using a "fact" we will tend to make decisions that are beneficial to us as individuals. The truth is, we like our will and the opportunity to exercise it. All of this is an expression of our self-centered nature.

God created us with a free will and throughout the Bible we are urged to exercise that free will to obey God and to love one another. We are told to love our neighbor as ourselves (Romans 13:9). The Bible tells us to evangelize others, to love one another and to obey God's commands. The Bible does not tell us that we should live our lives following only our own self-centered will.

Jonah is described in the Bible as a man who had little idea of what he wanted to do. But God had other plans for Jonah and pushed Jonah for obedience. Even when Jonah began to obey he was not happy. He had great success as an evangelist but his will still ran counter to God's will.

Our self-centered will was given to us by God to make good decisions governing our every day life. But that will is to be subservient to obedience to God. When God tells us to love one another but our will tells us that we only need to love ourselves, we have chosen our will over obedience.

If we are strong in our Christian faith, our will or obedience is an easy choice. We will choose obedience. When we do this we find that there is ample room for us to then follow our will within that obedience. Christians are the people with the greatest freedom of all people. God gives us certain commands and then we are told to live our lives within those commands giving us great amounts of freedom. God is with us as we make our decisions but we are allowed to make those decisions.

Seek obedience to God's commands and then God's will for your life. As a result, live the abundant life with joy within those commands and God's will.

STUDY QUESTIONS

1. What are God's commands? What are the most important ones?
2. What is God's will for your life?
3. Within God's commands and God's will for your life, what are your goals for the rest of your life (regardless of your age today)?

194

"As members of God's Kingdom, we're called to conquer the barriers between who we are and who God wants us to be." Pastor Dr. David Jeremiah

It is difficult to convince an intelligent person to change his or her mind but it is nearly impossible to change a person with a closed mind.

"Better to remain silent and be thought a fool, than to speak out and remove all doubt." Abraham Lincoln

"A new command I give you. Love one another. As I have loved you, so you must love one another." Jesus Christ Matthew 13:34

"I am the true vine, and my Father is the gardener. He cuts off every branch in me that bears no fruit, while every branch that does bear fruit He prunes so that it will be even more fruitful." John 15:1-2

"Repent and be baptized, every one of you, in the name of Jesus Christ for the forgiveness of your sins." Acts 2:38

UNFORGIVING SPIRIT

Do you have an unforgiving spirit? We all see ourselves as wronged at one time or another. It could have been unintentional but was likely intentional as seen by us. Our reaction to this tells much about us. We can remain unforgiving or we can forgive. But even if we say we forgive but harbor anger in our mind, have we really forgiven?

Ephesians 4:32 reads, "Be kind and compassionate to one another, forgiving each other, just as in Christ, God forgave you." <u>We are called to be forgiving of one another.</u> Our spirit, our nature, our attitude, tend to be one of when I am wronged, there must be restitution. At the very least, the offending party must ask for our forgiveness. But this is not what the Scripture says. When we are told to forgive, it does not state a number of conditions or describe what must happen with the offender.

An unforgiving spirit holds our anger, our bitterness within us. It holds us captive. We lose some of our freedom because we are limited by wanting to make sure no one thinks we are forgiving the offender. We begin to hold ourselves captive to our unforgiving spirit.

Freedom within our Christian faith means that we can love unconditionally all of God's creatures and all of what God has created. An unforgiving spirit means we say we love conditionally. We say we love except for those people we have not forgiven. We cannot love those we have not forgiven. This is contrary to what God has taught us. Our freedom means we can say I love everyone, even those who would do me harm. I love them because God created them. I might not love what they do or what they represent but I love unconditionally.

God loves us as is evident throughout the New Testament. All we need to do is ask for forgiveness which we need to do continually. What if God had an unforgiving spirit? That would void our ticket to Heaven. If God can forgive us our sins, why should we refrain from forgiving others?

In John 8:31 we are told that if we hold to the teachings of Jesus, we will be His disciples. Jesus adds, "Then you will know the truth, and the truth will set you free" (John 8:32). Jesus teaches us to forgive. If we forgive, we will know the truth and we will be free from the captivity of an unforgiving spirit.

STUDY QUESTIONS

1. Do you harbor an unforgiving spirit? What actions of others do you not forgive? Why are keeping this unforgiving spirit?
2. Has Jesus forgiven you for your many sins? What if Jesus had an unforgiving spirit?
3. Unconditional love to all gives us freedom from long-term anger. We don't have to approve of what others do or what they represent. But God did create them in His image. Can you forgive someone created in God's image?

278

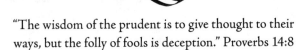

"The wisdom of the prudent is to give thought to their ways, but the folly of fools is deception." Proverbs 14:8

THE JOY OF BEING A CHRISTIAN

The Joy of Being A Christian should be evident in each of us. Each day we enter into the joy of the Lord. As we greet the day, our attitude should reflect Psalm 35:9 which reads, "Then my soul will rejoice in the Lord and delight in His salvation."

Every Christian should be joyful. There are many reasons. Here are some of them: 1) Joy means security in knowing where eternity will be spent, 2) Joy means the opportunity to spend time with others filled with joy (joy creates joy), 3) Spreading joy is a happy activity, 4) Spreading joy changes the lives of others, 5) Happy, peaceful people live longer, 6) Joy carries over into other parts of our lives, work, school, leisure, relationships, 7) Joy means discovering what is positive and enhancing it with praise, helpfulness, 8) Joy means even finding the best in a bad situation, 9) Joy means helping others, 10) Joy means being pleasing to God, 11) Joy helps others see our Christian faith in a positive way which can attract them to the faith, 12) Joy is productive, gets things done because a positive attitude produces more good results, and 13) Joy is healthy, when we are peace with the world our bodies have less stress.

As you consider this list, you will probably think of other reasons to be joyful. Write down what comes to mind. For me, part of the joy of going to church is seeing the joyful people I am able to greet there. If you can show a joyful countenance, others will become more joyful after greeting you.

But being joyful all of the day is not easy. There are many parts of life that draw us away from joy. We have to be diligent in maintaining our joy. We must recognize that: 1) Joy requires that we not let others drag us into their pessimism, anger or hate, 2) Joy requires that we keep the devil away (the devil loves a grumpy person), 3) Joy requires that we are forward looking, hoping for the best but prepared for the worst, 4) Joy requires that we take care of ourselves physically and mentally, 5) Joy requires that we have goals, things that we want to see happen (joy is hard to maintain when nothing positive is happening), and 6) Joy requires that we meet our responsibilities and accept opportunities carefully.

Psalm 66:1 tells us to "make a joyful noise unto the Lord" (KJV). Shortly before the ascension of Jesus, He told them "Receive the Holy Spirit" (John 20:22). In Gal 5:22 we are told that the fruit of the Spirit is "love, joy, peace, longsuffering, gentleness, goodness and faith" (KJV).

A "joyful noise" can be done in a spirit of peace with God. Billy Graham's book, *Peace with God*, addresses how we can seek this peace while at the same time make a "joyful noise" in combination to have the "Joy of Being a Christian." If you do not have this joy, stop to have some time in prayer to find this joy and peace. Today would be a good time. If you <u>have</u> this joy, share it with others.

STUDY QUESTIONS

1. Have you received the fruit of the Holy Spirit? Think about each part of the fruit as listed above in how in relates to your life today.
2. Consider 1 Peter 4:13. Write it out in your own words.
3. How joyful are you as the day passes? Are you able to control what we must be diligent about while maintaining your joy? See the list above and add others that you see as problems in remaining joyful.

419

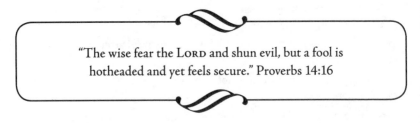

"The wise fear the LORD and shun evil, but a fool is hotheaded and yet feels secure." Proverbs 14:16

EGO AND SALVATION

Every person has an ego. It is what gives us the confidence to go about our day. Ideally, an ego is at a balance between being too strong and too weak. A weak ego means we are afraid to do most things because we are certain we will fail at them, people will ridicule us or that accomplishing the task will be meaningless anyway. An ego that is too strong tends to overwhelm others by wanting to control every situation including every conversation, causes talk only about self and makes us very conscious of the need to be at the center of attention in any activity. Control of a big ego is a reason men in particular have difficulty in becoming a Christian. At the same time, big egos are often a front for insecurity and fear.

We must give attention to the exhortation expressed by the Apostle Paul in Philippians 2:3-5: Do nothing out of selfish ambition or vain conceit. Rather, in humility value others above ourselves, not looking to our own interests but each of you to the interests of the others. In your relationships with one another, have the same mindset as Christ Jesus."

Each of us needs to achieve a balance in our ego. A balanced ego is based on true self-confidence. When we are self confident we know what we can do and do well. We feel good about ourselves without a lot of approval from others. We know who we are and are pleased with that role. At the same time, we have only a mild level of needing the approval of others and act when it is the right thing to do rather than acting because we think it might impress others or feed our ego.

Either extreme or lacking this balance in our ego makes it difficult to become a Christian. The person with little ego will be afraid to take any action and will not feel they are worth it anyway. The person with the big ego will find it difficult to accept that God is more important than they are. They are capable of worshiping only themselves and cannot accept any subservient role without a big dent in the ego.

Salvation means accepting John 3:16, that God sent his only son, Jesus Christ, to live on earth and then die on the cross for our sins. If we believe in Him and accept this forgiveness, we are promised eternal life in Heaven.

To accept this requires that we get our personal ego under control and in balance. Is your ego in balance so that you can accept the offer of salvation?

STUDY QUESTIONS

1. Describe your own ego. Is it in balance, too weak or too strong? If you are not sure, ask three friends to describe your ego to you.
2. If your ego needs adjustment, what are you going to do about it?
3. If your ego is in balance, have you made the commitment to accept John 3:16?

131

"The effects of life are 10% what happens to me and 90% how I react to it." Pastor Charles W. Swindoll

Ego is "the drug of nature to weaken the pain of being a fool." Pastor Dr. Davis Chappell

"There is nothing noble in being superior to your fellow men. True nobility lies in being superior to your former self." W. L. Sheldon (early 20th century ethicist)

FORGIVENESS

In order to be forgiven there must first be an act, oral or physical, for which we need to be forgiven. The Bible tells us (Romans 6, 7 and 8) that we are by nature sinful. As a result, all of us sin. The next step is to ask for forgiveness while understanding that forgiveness is given only when we admit to our sin and then ask for forgiveness. Being by nature sinful, it means that we continue to sin. Therefore, we must continually ask for forgiveness for our sins (John 1:9).

The act of asking for forgiveness means submitting ourselves to God. If our ego does not allow us to submit to God, we cannot ask for forgiveness. When we fail to ask for forgiveness, our sins are not forgiven. To state that we are sorry for committing a sin might only mean that we are sorry that we were caught in sin or that we regret having done or said something. It is a much bigger step to ask God and fellow man for forgiveness. This is because forgiveness is more than regret, it is more than admission, it means asking God and our fellow man to do something. That act on the part of God and our fellow man is accepting our request for forgiveness. That is an act of mercy on the part of God who is willing to wipe the slate clean. That sin is then no longer a barrier between the sinner and God. Consider Paul who killed Christians. God forgave him.

Asking for forgiveness is more than simply stopping the sin. Asking for forgiveness is more than saying I am sorry. It is more than saying I will not do this again. Forgiveness relates to what has already happened, the sin that has already been committed. Forgiveness is setting the situation straight by asking for forgiveness. The difference is that an individual might not be as merciful as God in granting forgiveness.

Asking for forgiveness becomes complete when God accepts the request for forgiveness as genuine and forgives us. Except for the sin of blasphemy (sinning against God), God forgives every sin but only if we ask and do so with a contrite heart, with genuineness. We also need to ask those affected or aware of our sin for forgiveness. Psalm 32:1 adds: "Blessed is the one whose transgressions are forgiven, whose sins are covered."

Once we are forgiven by God and man, we are not free of future sin because of our sinful nature. Once forgiven we need to seek restitution of our position before the sin. This could take time when trust or relationships need to be rebuilt. When we sin, we must acknowledge our sin and then ask for forgiveness in all sincerity. We can be forgiven only if we are willing to humble ourselves to ask for that forgiveness. Have you asked for forgiveness today? Are you willing to forgive others?

STUDY QUESTIONS

1. Acknowledge a sin that you have committed in the past week. Have you specifically asked God for forgiveness for this sin?
2. When a person sins against you, are you willing to accept their request for forgiveness? This can be the beginning of a restoration of a relationship.
3. Are there sins in the past for which you have publicly expressed regret but you did not humble yourself before God to ask for forgiveness?

188

"You can't ask for the forgiveness of someone else's sins, only your own."

"Our activities need to be in balance with our prioritized goals or the outcomes will be a disappointment." Anonymous

"Repent of this wickedness and pray to the Lord in the hope that he may forgive you for having such a thought in your heart" Acts 8:22

"For if you forgive other people when they sin against you, your heavenly Father will also forgive you" Matthew 6:14

THE GREATEST CHRISTMAS GIFT

The Greatest Christmas Gift was predicted in the Old Testament when the prophet Isaiah in Chapter 9:6-7 of Isaiah, said: "For to us a child is born, to us a son is given, and the government will be on his shoulders. And he will be called Wonderful Counselor, Mighty God, Everlasting Father, Prince of Peace. Of the greatness of his government and peace there will be no end."

Do you remember a Christmas when you were promised a gift that you wanted? <u>This</u> greatest Christmas gift of all was promised to each of us centuries before we were even born. But like all gifts, we have to <u>accept</u> it. Doesn't it sound strange that the greatest Christmas gift of all is not accepted by so many while others acknowledge it, yet put it aside thinking very little about it? Think about how this greatest Christmas gift has changed your life.

This greatest Christmas gift has two parts. One is described in John 3:16 and 17 in the New Testament where it tells us that "For God so loved the world that he gave his one and only Son, that whoever believes in Him shall not perish but have eternal life. For God did not send His Son into the world to condemn the world, but to save the world through Him." So God sent his one and only Son to us because He loved us and then offered eternal life to those who would accept the gift, his Son. Eternal life in Heaven is put into perspective when we consider that there is only one other alternative, eternal life in Hell. No person in his or her right mind would want to go to Hell, particularly for eternity. Instead, we can accept the greatest Christmas gift and spend eternity in Heaven when life on earth is over. Do you acknowledge the fact that God has offered this gift?

And there is more. The second part of the greatest Christmas gift is an offer to help us while on this earth, while this life continues. We all face temptation, sadness and indecision. How we can deal with those challenges on earth is described in Ephesians 6:13 which reads, "Therefore, put on the full armor of God, so that when the day of evil comes, you may be able to stand your ground, and after you have done everything, to stand." God is here through his son, Jesus Christ, and the Holy Spirit to help us face the worst of situations on earth. But this part of the greatest Christmas gift also has to be <u>accepted</u> in order to help us. Are you willing to acknowledge and then accept the greatest Christmas gift?

STUDY QUESTIONS

1. What is the most cherished Christmas gift that a person gave to you in the past? How does it compare to the gift of salvation?
2. Consider that the greatest gift you might ever give at any time would be to help someone accept Jesus Christ, God's greatest gift.
3. How might you show your appreciation to God for offering the greatest Christmas gift to you?

175

"She will give birth to a son, and you are to give him the name Jesus, because He will save His people from their sins" Matthew 1:21

"For God so loved the world that He gave His one and only Son, that whoever believes in Him shall not perish but have everlasting life" John 3:16

GOD WILL TAKE CARE OF YOU

God will take care of us. There are two songs that come to mind on this topic. One of them is God Will Take Care of You. Written in 1904 by Civilla D. Martin, the words to the song are:

> Be not dismayed what'er betide,
> God will take care of you.
> Beneath His wings of love abide,
> God will take care of you.
> Refrain: God will take care of you,
> Through every day, o'er all the way;
> He will take care of you,
> God will take care of you.

Matthew 6:25 tells us ", do not worry about your life, what you will eat or drink, or about your body, what you will wear." In 1 Peter 5:7 we are told, "Cast all your anxiety on Him because he cares for you." Jesus said, "Why are ye fearful, O ye of little faith." (Mt 8:26 KJV). "But seek first His kingdom and his righteousness and all these things will be given to you as well" (Mt 6:33).

In 1905 Civilla D. Martin wrote the other song about God taking care of us. The title is His Eye Is on the Sparrow. The words to this song are:

> Why should I feel discouraged, why should the shadows come?
> Why should my heart be lonely, and long for heav'n and home?
> When Jesus is my portion? My constant friend is He:
> His eye is on the sparrow, and I know He watches me;
> His eye is on the sparrow, and I know He watches me.
> Refrain: I sing because I'm happy, I sing because I'm free,
> For His eye is on the sparrow, and I know He watches me.

In Matthew 6:26 Jesus states "Look at the birds of the air; they do not sow or reap or store away in barns, and yet your Heavenly Father feeds them.

Are you not much more valuable than they?" If we truly seek His Kingdom first and are believers in the Bible and accept the salvation described in John 3:16, we will continue to have life's ups and downs but we will know that our lives in Heaven are assured. Have you taken that step to let God take care of you?

STUDY QUESTIONS

1. Are you already a Christian? Do you accept God's direction for your life and then trust in Him to take care of you?
2. Compare yourself to the sparrow in the song or in Matthew 6:26. Birds of the air have food and water without doing anything to create or conserve it. God loves us even more. Do you trust Him?
3. Why do we worry? Can we both worry and trust God?

234

"Therefore, we must give the more earnest heed to the things we have heard, lest we drift away" Hebrews 2:1

"He who testifies to these things says, 'Surely I am coming quickly.' Amen. Even so, come, Lord Jesus! The grace of our Lord Jesus Christ be with you all. Amen" Revelation 22:20-21

"My sheep listen to my voice; I know them, and they follow me. I give them eternal life, and they shall never perish; no one can snatch them out of my hand" John 10:27

"These have come so that the proven genuineness of your faith – of greater worth than gold, which perishes even though refined by fire – may result in praise, glory and honor when Jesus Christ is revealed" 1 Peter 1:7

"For you know that it was not with perishable things such as silver or gold that you were redeemed from the empty way of life handed down to you from your ancestors, but with the precious blood of Christ, a lamb without blemish or defect" 1 Peter 1:18

"Wisdom reposes in the heart of the discerning and even among fools she lets herself be known." Proverbs 14:33

"You won't learn to be obedient with a closed Bible." Pastor Dr. Adrian Rogers

Wisdom will come to us in many forms and from many different sources. Often we do not recognize the wisdom and sometimes we refuse to acknowledge it because it runs against our own bias toward what we think is true. There could be some wisdom that does not apply to us at the moment but should still be understood so that it might be applied when the opportunity arrives. None of us is fully prepared for all of the experiences we will face in life but the more we are ready to apply wisdom principles to new situations, the more likely it is that we will have positive outcomes.

While we accept wisdom from the Bible for where it applies, the words of man are often offered as wisdom but might be the opposite. We must carefully discern whether advice we receive is consistent with our Christian faith and other values. When it is, we are to help others by disseminating wisdom that could be helpful to others. When it is not, we should challenge what is being said.

Probably our greatest opportunity to apply wisdom is in our own lives. A statement of wisdom is a principle. A principle guides us in many situations as we apply it to the specific circumstances. Looking at problems and opportunities without principles means we might have very different outcomes for similar situations over time because the prevalent factors instead of principles are likely to be emotion, pressure from others, the physical surrounding, fear, jealousy, pride, arrogance and/or stupidity (action without thinking). The more situations we can face to which we can apply wisdom principles, the more we will please God, others we impact and ourselves.

One of the purposes of this book is to raise consciousness of the wisdom principles that are available to us. There are many more wisdom principles. The wise person learns from others through reading, listening and discussion. The wise person seeks out wisdom that he or she can utilize now and in the future. The wise person understands the wisdom principles and puts them to use in life every day.

What wisdom principles have direct or indirect application to your life today?

God's Plan for Service